LATIMER STUDIES 78

FOR US AND FOR OUR SALVATION

'LIMITED ATONEMENT' IN THE BIBLE, DOCTRINE, HISTORY, AND MINISTRY

BY LEE GATISS

The Latimer Trust

For Us and For Our Salvation: 'Limited Atonement' in the Bible, Doctrine, History, and Ministry © Lee Gatiss 2012

ISBN 978-1-906327-07-1

Cover photo: yellow tulip © Lisa Turay – Fotolia.com

Unless otherwise indicated, Scripture quotations are the author's own translation. Those marked NIV are from The Holy Bible, New International Version (Anglicised edition), copyright © 1979, 1984, 2011 by Biblica (formerly International Bible Society). Used by permission of Hodder & Stoughton Publishers, an Hachette UK company. All rights reserved. 'NIV' is a registered trademark of Biblica (formerly International Bible Society). UK trademark number 1448790.

Quotations from 'O Church, Arise' by Keith Getty and Stuart Townend and 'Beautiful Saviour' by Stuart Townend are used with permission. Adm. by worshiptogether.com songs excl. UK & Europe, adm. by Kingswaysongs, a division of David C Cook. tym@kingsway.co.uk.

Published by the Latimer Trust May 2012

The Latimer Trust (formerly Latimer House, Oxford) is a conservative Evangelical research organisation within the Church of England, whose main aim is to promote the history and theology of Anglicanism as understood by those in the Reformed tradition. Interested readers are welcome to consult its website for further details of its many activities.

The Latimer Trust
c/o Oak Hill College
London N14 4PS UK
Registered Charity: 1084337
Company Number: 4104465
Web: www.latimertrust.org
E-mail: administrator@latimertrust.org

CONTENTS

'This book is a masterful, mini-treatise on the characteristically Reformed view of God's purpose and achievement in the cross of Christ that goes by the name of limited atonement or particular or definite redemption. The author knows his way around, and his deployment of exegetical, historical and pastoral evidence adds up to a very full case of his position. The question is more important than is sometimes realised and I heartily commend this clear-headed, warm-hearted treatment of it.'

J.I. Packer,
Board of Governors' Professor of Theology,
Regent College, Vancouver.

'Limited atonement is often described by those who reject it as "a textless doctrine" and thus dismissed. Lee Gatiss here offers a clear and succinct exposition of the concept, showing how scripture, theology, and church history all offer a powerful cumulative case for the doctrine of particular redemption. This is an excellent introduction to the topic, setting forth the positive while handling objections with care and respect.'

Carl Trueman,
Professor of Historical Theology and Church History,
Westminster Theological Seminary, Philadelphia

'This little book blends careful and extensive research with accessibility. Even those who remain unconvinced of the biblical and theological credentials of limited atonement as it is popularly taught must abandon caricature and agree that its advocates are conscientious exegetes who take the cosmic scope of God's purposes seriously and can also be passionate evangelists. Those who are committed to this position will discover their debating partners are not all proof-texters with no regard for logical or theological consistency but instead have valid concerns which should be addressed rather than parodied. This often far too heated a debate needs some serious cooling. Here is a largely successful attempt to provide an even-handed and irenic introduction to the issues. Wherever you stand you will benefit from reading this book.'

Mark D. Thompson,
Head of Theology,
Moore Theological College, Sydney

'Every page a feast of good things! I defy anyone to read this book without finding it easy and informative, with something to feed the mind and warm the heart on each page. Whether, in part one, concentrating on exegesis of texts, or, in part two, surveying historical theology, or, in part three, drawing out practical implications. Gatiss writes in a comfortably readable style, deploys a covetable breadth of reading and a mastery of his subject, and preserves an irenically gracious spirit. The centrally important topic of "limited atonement" could not be more persuasively or helpfully presented.'

Alec Motyer,
Old Testament Editor of *The Bible Speaks Today* series

'The last thing Lee Gatiss wants to accomplish by this short book is to renew theological conflict characterized by more heat than light. Rather, Gatiss makes his case patiently, respectfully, firmly - beginning with Scripture, traversing historical and systematic theology, and ending with pastoral reflections. Those who disagree will find themselves much better informed; those who are sympathetic to the argument and who understand the biblical and theological connections between definite atonement and penal substitution will rejoice to see the case freshly made. After all, it draws believers to the foot of the cross in humility and stunned awe before the Redeemer whose perfect obedience accomplished the wise and gracious plan of our Creator and Judge. While he works through the details of text and logic, Gatiss does not lose sight of the massive and central place of the cross in the panoramic biblical display of God's redemptive purposes.'

D.A. Carson,
Research Professor of New Testament,
Trinity Evangelical Divinity School, Deerfield, Illinois

'Lee Gatiss has given us perhaps the most thorough examination of the doctrine of limited atonement in decades. Few stones are left unturned and a compelling case is mounted. The argument is well-nuanced and the author tries carefully to avoid tribal extremism or strained exegesis. His closing section on how preachers phrase their explanations of the cross in evangelism is worth careful pondering.'

Julian Hardyman,
Senior Pastor, Eden Baptist Church, Cambridge

'Lee Gatiss has given us an extraordinarily rich resource for thinking through a specific question: the scope of Christ's saving work. He recognizes that the question, "For *whom* did Christ die?" is inseparably bound up with the more crucial question, "What did he *accomplish* in his death?" Drawing together scriptural exegesis and historical debates, this book dispels caricatures and displays the strength and relevance of this doctrine for the church today. Regardless of where the reader stands on particular redemption, *For Us and For Our Salvation* will be an indispensable resource for understanding the biblical arguments and historical issues.'

Michael S. Horton,
Professor of Systematic Theology and Apologetics,
Westminster Theological Seminary, California

'To my shame, I have never seriously looked at limited atonement. It was a jaw-dropping realisation for me when this book explained the implications of the doctrine. As the book examined all of the most relevant scripture texts, my personal conviction grew that God's overwhelming and overflowing grace could never be expressed by limited atonement. But I must read it again and – more to the point – I must read all the scriptures again. This book has, if nothing else, made me think about biblical theology in an important area that I had neglected.'

David Instone-Brewer,
Senior Research Fellow in Rabbinics and the New Testament,
Tyndale House, Cambridge.

Acknowledgements

I would like to take this opportunity to thank those who have been particularly important in my on-going quest for clarity and truth on this subject (which I confess has not always been easy and will no doubt continue). My wife Kerry has patiently endured many debates in our living room about it and has always been a reassuring support in the face of the adversity that sometimes comes from sticking one's neck out. She also put her own not insubstantial biblical, theological, and pastoral skills to work in commenting on an early draft of this book.

Pride of place must also go to my old friend David Gibbs, whose keen mind and godly pastoral heart helped me begin to wrestle with the issue in earnest about 15 years ago. Others who have been especially helpful in various ways, including via disagreement, include Mike Horton (who first introduced me to limited atonement at an RTSF talk in Oxford in the early 1990s), Gerald Bray, Richard Muller, Ben Cooper, Ro Mody, Garry Williams, Paul Darlington, Steve Walton, Pete Sanlon, John Telford, Timothy Edwards, Carl Chambers, Jonny Gibson, Richard Snoddy, Marty Foord, Mark Thompson, Michael Jensen, Michael Lynch, and David Ponter, as well as Dick Lucas, Jonathan Fletcher, and William Taylor.

This book was substantially drafted five years ago, but I was not able to publish it then. In the meantime, however, I have been blessed by the feedback of these and other people as it has circulated in draft form. I have quite deliberately sought out the most penetrating and detailed criticisms of successive drafts that I could. In particular, I owe a huge debt to those who have at different times expressed varying levels of discomfort with doctrines of particular redemption and were generous with their time and energy in discussion and correspondence. I have benefited immensely from personal interaction with such learned interlocutors. Even if they still may not be in agreement with every word I have written, I hope this book is all the better for the extra effort I had to put into reading and thinking about what they said and trying to address their concerns through literally hundreds of amendments, both large and small. The saying is trustworthy: as iron sharpens iron so one man sharpens another (Proverbs 27:17). I hope they have benefited from the experience as much as I have.

All translations from the Bible and other foreign language sources are my own unless otherwise stated. Thanks to Kylie Thomas and Gerald Bray at Tyndale House in Cambridge, and Dr. Robert Crellin at the Greek Bible Institute in Athens, for casting their expert eyes over some of my Latin and French translations. Any errors that remain can, of course, only be in those sections which I did not pass under their noses. Thanks also to Robin Mark for permission to use some lines from his song 'Lion of Judah.'

I do not pretend that I have all the answers or that what I have written is the last word on this subject. Nor am I attempting to raise it into a new shibboleth or give it unwarranted prominence. I do hope, however, that this short book will contribute in a positive and irenic way to further friendly exchanges in the future. As always, however, I pray that the result will be 'less heat, more light,' as we humbly submit together to the unerring word of God in all our imperfect and limited theologising. *Soli Deo gloria.*

LEE GATISS

Cambridge

INTRODUCTION

In their recent high profile book on the cross Steve Jeffery, Mike Ovey, and Andrew Sach include a few pages which address the subject of what is classically called 'limited atonement.'[1] They very helpfully attempt to answer various objections to the classic evangelical doctrine that Jesus died to take the punishment our sins deserve from God. One objection runs like this: 'Penal Substitution implies universal salvation, which is unbiblical.' The authors carefully reveal the hidden assumption in this statement, which is that Jesus died for all people. So, the thinking goes, if penal substitution is true, surely all people are saved from ever bearing the wrath of God themselves? Their answer (like that of many theologians over the centuries) is a version of limited atonement: that Jesus died only for those who were chosen.

How the cross can be both 'unlimited' *and* truly substitutionary without this leading to universal salvation is a common question. It comes up in a number of contexts, from theological college essays to evangelistic conversations with intelligent non-believers. It is thus an eminently reasonable topic for discussion in a book on penal substitution and takes up only 10 or so pages out of over 300 in *Pierced for our Transgressions*.[2] This issue has, however, taken up a great deal more space in reviews and discussion of that book since then: the review in *Christianity* magazine, for instance, devoted about half its space to criticism of these few pages.[3]

---

[1] S. Jeffery, M. Ovey, and A. Sach, *Pierced for our Transgressions: Rediscovering the Glory of Penal Substitution* (Leicester: IVP, 2007), pp 268-278.

[2] Since the authors of *Pierced for our Transgressions* were all associated with Oak Hill Theological College it is not surprising that they felt the need to address this subject somewhere. A former lecturer at Oak Hill, Dr. Martin Davie, created a furore there in 1999 by publicly denying penal substitution in his (unpublished) Tyndale Fellowship Doctrine Lecture, 'Dead to Sin and Alive to God' which ended by devoting over 1500 words to the subject of limited atonement.

[3] http://www.christianitymagazine.co.uk/reviews/books/pierced%20for%20our%20transgressions.aspx.

The extent of the atonement, therefore, continues to be 'one of the most controversial teachings in Reformed soteriology.'[4]   In the past it was the focus of intense debate with very practical consequences: General and Particular Baptists split over the issue in the seventeenth century,[5] and Calvinistic Baptists were divided over the approach to the atonement of the famous Kettering minister, Andrew Fuller (1754–1815).[6] Controversy often raged over this subject within evangelical circles in Wales,[7] and in Scotland ministers have been tried for heresy on it, such as John Macleod Campbell of the Church of Scotland in the early nineteenth century.[8] Indeed, Macleod Campbell's book *The Nature of the Atonement* first published in 1856 spearheaded opposition to limited atonement from *within* the Reformed camp.[9] Today, neo-orthodox Barthians reject it,[10] as do many within the conservative evangelical fold – not just classic Arminians but also Calvinists, many following the lead of the great Australian theologian David

---

[4]   R.A. Blacketer, 'Definite Atonement in Historical Perspective' in C.E. Hill and F.A. James (eds.), *The Glory of the Atonement: Biblical, Theological, and Practical Perspectives* (Downers Grove: IVP, 2004), p 304.

[5]   See T. George, *Theology of the Reformers* (Leicester: Apollos, 1988), p 233 and G. Beynon, 'The Rise and Development of the English Baptists' at http://www.theologian.org.uk/churchhistory/englishbaptists.html.

[6]   See W. Rushton, *Particular Redemption and the Theology of Andrew Fuller* (Eggleston: Go Publications, 2006).

[7]   See the detailed look at this in O. Thomas, *The Atonement Controversy in Welsh Theological Literature and Debate, 1707-1841* (Edinburgh: Banner of Truth, 2002).

[8]   See G.M. Tuttle, *So Rich an Soil: John McLeod Campbell on Christian Atonement* (Edinburgh: Handsel Press, 1986) and J.C. Goodloe, *John McLeod Campbell: The Extent and Nature of the Atonement* (Princeton: Princeton Theological Seminary, 1997).

[9]   According to Blacketer, 'Definite Atonement', p 305. See J. McLeod Campbell, *The Nature of the Atonement and its Relation to Remission of Sins and Eternal Life* (London: Macmillian, 1869).

[10]   See, for example, J.B. Torrance, 'The Incarnation and "Limited Atonement"' in *Scottish Bulletin of Evangelical Theology* 2 (1984) and T. Hart, 'Humankind in Christ and Christ in Humankind: Salvation as Participation in Our Substitute in the Theology of John Calvin' in *Scottish Journal of Theology* 42 (1989).

Broughton Knox and indeed of the influential nineteenth century Bishop, J.C. Ryle.[11]

Studying this topic is a challenging exercise, requiring as it does an integration of biblical exegesis, an awareness of historical and systematic theology, and pastoral implications. In addition, it can also reveal a great deal about one's presuppositions on methodological questions. For instance, some profess to dislike limited atonement because it is 'too neat', as if consistency and coherence in doctrinal formulation necessarily equates to falsity. Others, claiming to follow the Bible alone, object to 'systems' and the use of logic in formulating doctrine. R.T. Kendall speaks for many when he asserts that 'At the end of the day all that matters is what the Scriptures say... I can safely guarantee that the traditional doctrine of limited atonement is arrived at by logic and the need to look for it rather than straightforward reading of the Scriptures.'[12] Others baulk emotionally at particularity in the scheme of salvation generally, while some are reluctant to accept it pragmatically because of certain apparent implications, such as the conclusion that if the atonement is not universal then one cannot exhort unbelievers to come to Christ by saying, 'he died for you'.

In this study, therefore, we will survey biblical, historical, and doctrinal arguments over limited atonement with an eye to the implications these might have on the practice of ministry and evangelism. First, we will attempt to define the question to which limited atonement is supposed to be the answer. Then, since doctrine must be built on exegesis, we will examine the biblical basis

---

[11] Knox's views are well summarised in 'Some Aspects of the Atonement' in T. Payne (ed.), *D. Broughton Knox, Selected Works* (Kingsford: Matthias Media, 2000), 1: pp 260-266. Ryle's views are expressed in J.C. Ryle, *Expository Thoughts on John* (Edinburgh: Banner of Truth, 1987), 1: pp 61-62 (on John 1:29). John Stott may also be added to this number if we regard his brief comments in *The Cross of Christ* (Leicester: IVP, 1989), p 147 as indicative of his mind on the larger issue. Cf. his carefully ambiguous comments in *The Letters of John* (Leicester: IVP, 1988), p 89.

[12] R.T. Kendall, *Calvin and English Calvinism to 1649* (Carlisle: Paternoster, 1997), viii. Ironically, on page 212 Kendall accuses 'Westminster theology' of being 'haunted with inconsistencies' and thus criticizes Calvinists for not being as logically consistent as he who is apparently so unconcerned with logical consistency!

of the arguments for and against it in scripture. Third, we will survey some historical and doctrinal areas of dispute: the pre-Reformation roots of the doctrine; the debate over Calvin's position; the Synod of Dort; and whether there is such a thing as an official Anglican stance on the subject. In conclusion, we will look at some practical implications of the doctrine.

This is not intended to be an exhaustive and comprehensive examination of every single detail in the debate. Such a work would easily run into several hundred pages. What I hope to provide, however, is an overview of the main contours of the exegetical, theological, and historical debates so that those who wish to dig deeper into them can do so with a sense of the lie of the land. In my experience, many discussions of this topic quickly flounder, or become unnecessarily heated, because participants are not adequately aware of some key ingredients of the classic positions. We should be able to have gracious but robust debate of theological questions like this without deteriorating into cheap sloganeering, ignorant name-calling, or gross misrepresentation. My hope and prayer is that an in-depth briefing will help raise the quality of argument in this area.

Naturally I am not claiming to be entirely neutral or dispassionate about this subject (both of which are sinful when it comes to our attitude to the truth). It is vitally important, however, not to generate more heat than light in our discussions. In my view, although I believe it to be clearly in error, the doctrine of unlimited or universal atonement is not a 'heresy' in and of itself, nor is this something over which Reformed evangelicals should seriously fall out.[13] John Davenant, a British delegate at the Synod of Dort, wrote: 'We had a special Charge in our Instructions to endeavour that *Positions* be moderately laid down, which may tend to the mitigation of heat on both parts, which we judge to be most necessary,'

---

[13] B.G. Armstrong's book, *Calvinism and the Amyraut Heresy: Protestant Scholasticism and Humanism in Seventeenth Century France* (Madison: University of Wisconsin Press, 1969) is badly named, since Amyraut's view of the atonement was not considered 'heresy' by other Reformed scholars at the time, in the way Arminianism was.

particularly on this subject.[14] King James instructed the British delegates to be especially careful when 'there be many oppositions between any who are overmuch addicted to their own opinions.'[15] This is wise counsel on what can still be a touchy subject, and I intend seriously to take note of it in both the tone and content of what follows.

---

[14] J. Davenant, 'Doctour Davenant touching the Second Article, discussed at the conference at the Haghe of the Extent of Redemption' in A. Milton (ed.), *The British Delegation and the Synod of Dort* (Woodbridge, Suffolk: Boydell Press, 2005), p 222.

[15] See 'Instructions of King James I to the delegates' in Milton, *British Delegation*, p 94 (updated spelling).

7

I.   DEFINING THE QUESTION

To begin, we must see if we can define the precise question at issue. Louis Berkhof succinctly summarises the issue:

> The question with which we are concerned at this point is not (a) whether the satisfaction rendered by Christ was in itself sufficient for the salvation of all men, since this is admitted by all; (b) whether the saving benefits are actually applied to every man, for the great majority of those who teach a universal atonement do not believe that all are actually saved; (c) whether the *bona fide* offer of salvation is made to all that hear the gospel, on the condition of repentance and faith, since the Reformed Churches do not call this in question; nor (d) whether any of the fruits of the death of Christ accrue to the benefit of the non-elect in virtue of their close association with the people of God, since this is explicitly taught by many Reformed scholars.   On the other hand, the question does relate to the design of the atonement.   Did the Father in sending Christ, and did Christ in coming into the world, to make atonement for sin, *do this with the design or for the purpose of saving only the elect or all men?*   That is the question, and that only is the question.[1]

This is the standard definition of the question from a Reformed point of view,[2] and very effectively distinguishes the Calvinist doctrine from the Arminian and Amyraldian alternatives, as those opposed to limited atonement have also conceded.[3] Berkhof is patently correct in

---

[1]   L. Berkhof, *Systematic Theology* (Edinburgh: Banner of Truth, 1981), pp 393-394.

[2]   See how the question is defined in terms of design, intent, or purpose in F. Turretin, *Institutes of Elenctic Theology* (Phillipsburg: P&R, 1994), 2.14.XIV.ix-xi on pp 458-459; C. Hodge, *Systematic Theology* (Peabody: Hendrickson, [1871] 1999), 2: pp 544-545; L. Boettner, *The Reformed Doctrine of Predestination* (Phillipsburg: P&R, 1932), p 150; J. Murray, 'The Atonement and the Free Offer of the Gospel' in *Collected Writings of John Murray* (Edinburgh: Banner of Truth, 1976), 1: p 63 which says there is also advantage in using the language of 'extent'; and R. Nicole, *Our Sovereign Saviour: The Essence of the Reformed Faith* (Fearn: Christian Focus, 2002), pp 58-60.

[3]   E.g. R.P. Lightner, *The Death Christ Died: A Biblical Case for Unlimited Atonement* (Grand Rapids: Kregel, 1998), pp 33-34.

what he denies here. As Henri Blocher says, 'Counterarguments usually fail to perceive the logic of "definite atonement" and what it consistently allows, that is, sufficiency for all, universal offer, salvation accomplished for the 'race' as an organic whole, and the like.'[4]

We might also add that the question is not about whether God loves all that he has made or only has time for the elect. No - 'The LORD is good to all, and his mercies are over all his works' (Psalm 145:9). As Matthew 5:44-45 suggests, we should love our enemies because God loves all, making the sun rise on the evil and the good and sending rain to both as well. The Lord Jesus displayed a deep, gut-wrenching compassion for the masses (Matthew 9:36). Several theologians have very effectively shown that scripture can speak of God's love in different ways so that an advocate of limited atonement (or of predestination) can still affirm that, in some sense, God loves everyone in the world.[5] As Geerhardus Vos, an advocate of limited atonement, put it, '[t]hat God loves the world in its natural existence, even outside the sphere of the covenant, contains a pledge of the bestowal upon the same world of an infinitely higher redemptive love.'[6] This universal love is not the same as his redemptive special love for his elect, which is the type of love most emphasized in scripture.[7] We must be careful not to relegate God's special love for the elect to a secondary stage in God's decree and thus

---

[4] H. Blocher, 'The Atonement in John Calvin's Theology' in Hill and James, *The Glory of the Atonement*, pp 280-281. In context, Blocher is particularly warning against misinterpreting Calvin.

[5] See D.A. Carson, *The Difficult Doctrine of the Love of God* (Leicester: IVP, 2000), pp 17-27 where he distinguishes five ways in which the Bible speaks of God's love. See also Murray, 'The Atonement and the Free Offer', pp 69-72; J.I. Packer, 'The Love of God: Universal and Particular' in T. R. Schreiner & B. A. Ware (eds.), *Still Sovereign: Contemporary Perspectives on Election, Foreknowledge, and Grace* (Grand Rapids: Baker, 2000), pp 282-284.

[6] See G. Vos, 'The Scriptural Doctrine of the Love of God' in R.B. Gaffin (ed.), *Redemptive History and Biblical Interpretation: The Shorter Writings of Geerhardus Vos* (Phillipsburg: P&R, 1980), p 442.

[7] Out of many many possibilities, we might consider here passages such as Deuteronomy 4:37, 5:10, 7:7-13, 10:15, 23:5, 33:3 or Malachi 1:2-3, 'I have loved you... I loved Jacob, but I hated Esau', as well as the fact that those who are 'loved by God' in the New Testament are specifically members of the churches (e.g. Romans 1:7, 1 Thessalonians 1:4, 2 Thessalonians 2:13, Jude 1).

make it an afterthought (as Arminian and Amyraldian presentations often do) but maintain the proper biblical 'distribution of emphasis.'[8]

Moreover, as John Frame suggests, 'The point at issue here is not whether God wants all men to be saved if they believe. (Of course he does!)'.[9] Jesus is very clear: 'All that the Father gives me will come to me, and the one who comes to me I will never cast out' (John 6:37). It is apparent here, however, that as Don Carson puts it, 'Jesus' confidence does not rest in the potential for positive response amongst well-meaning people. Far from it: his confidence is in his Father to bring to pass the Father's redemptive purposes.'[10] The elect *will* come, and he will keep them, so that 'if you confess with your mouth, "Jesus is Lord" and believe in your heart that God raised him from the dead, you will be saved' (Romans 10:9). Often the problem people have with this doctrine is the related thought that God does not give everyone to Jesus, that is, he does not secure the ultimate salvation of everyone. Yet this is really a problem further back, with the idea of predestination, not with the atonement *per se*. It needs to be addressed at that level first. I will not here defend the doctrine that God unconditionally chooses some people (and not others), because that would itself require a whole book. What we are exploring here is, more narrowly, the relationship between predestination and the cross.

Wayne Grudem takes issue with Berkhof's narrowing of the atonement question. He says that to focus on God's purpose in the atonement is to make this 'just another form of the larger dispute between Calvinists and Arminians' over whether God's plan is to save those he has chosen or to save everybody (a plan frustrated by the exercise of free will).[11] Since it was indeed an Arminian challenge which drew out the classic definition of limited atonement at the Synod of Dort, this seems to be a strange criticism. Other questions could be used as a way in to the debate: as the Palatinate delegation suggested at Dort, 'the whole question concerns the efficiency and

---

[8] Cf. Vos, 'The Scriptural Doctrine', p 456.
[9] J. Frame, review of *Calvinism and the Amyraut Heresy* in *Westminster Theological Journal* 34:2 (May 1972), p 190. He adduces 2 Peter 3:9 in support.
[10] D.A. Carson, *The Gospel According to John* (Leicester: IVP, 1991), p 290.
[11] W. Grudem, *Systematic Theology: An Introduction to Biblical Doctrine* (Leicester: IVP, 1994), p 601.

efficacy of the ransom."[12] In other words, is redemption effective actually to save people or does the cross merely render us potentially saveable (if we meet certain conditions, like having faith)? Indeed, the contention of those who believe in unlimited atonement has often been that Christ's death does not save either actually or potentially; rather it makes everyone saveable.[13]

One commentator claims that it is foreign to Arminianism to say 'Christ paid the penalty for our sins,' that is, that Arminians do not truly believe in penal substitutionary atonement. This is because 'Arminians teach that what Christ did he did for every person; therefore what he did could not have been to pay the penalty, since no one would then ever go into eternal perdition... They understand that there can be only punishment or forgiveness, not both."[14] This connects the issue of the extent of the atonement with the actual nature of the atonement itself (is it a penal substitution, or not?). It is indeed hard to disentangle all these issues from election and the rest of the Calvinist-Arminian debate. But we should note that many Arminians are happy to affirm penal substitution while others are not, having a more Grotian 'governmental' view of the atonement.[15]

I do not think the question can be re-phrased, '*how much* did Christ die for people?' in a quantitative sense. It is not as if the atonement was 'stuff' that can be mechanically limited in amount

---

[12] G.M. Thomas, *The Extent of the Atonement: A Dilemma for Reformed Theology from Calvin to the Consensus* (Carlisle: Paternoster, 1997), p 135. Grudem, *Systematic Theology*, p 597 agrees that the central issue is the efficacy of the atonement.

[13] See Lewis Sperry Chafer, 'For Whom Did Christ Die?' *Bibliotheca Sacra* 137 (Oct-Dec 1980) and his *Systematic Theology* (Dallas: Dallas Theological Seminary, 1948), 3: p 193. R. Olson, *Arminian Theology: Myths and Realities* (Downers Grove: IVP, 2006), p 222 says 'Arminians believe that Christ's death on the cross provided *possible* salvation for everyone' (emphasis original). J. van Genderen and W. H. Velema, *Concise Reformed Dogmatics* (Phillipsburg: P&R, 2008), p 526 refer to this as a 'possibility-realization scheme.'

[14] J.K. Grider, 'Arminianism' in W.A. Elwell, *Evangelical Dictionary of Theology* (Grand Rapids: Baker, 1984), p 80.

[15] See the careful differentiation of various Arminian views in Olson, *Arminian Theology*, pp 221-241. Hugo Grotius was a major figure in seventeenth century Arminianism, so his view is often called '*the* Arminian view' although Arminius' own position was somewhat different to Grotius'. Both have been held by those who call themselves Arminians since.

and distributed in parcels to only a restricted number of people. It is not as if each minute on the cross or millilitre of blood was worth 1,000 sins or some such commercial calculation.[16] It seems better to say that the atonement was qualitative in that if, for the sake of argument, God decided to elect one more person post-crucifixion, Christ would not have to go back to the cross for a few minutes more suffering, or to die again. His one death had infinite worth, because of who he is, and the wages of sin is death (Romans 6:23) not a certain amount or intensity of suffering *per se*.[17] A sacrifice of infinite worth is necessary for the salvation of one sinner or every sinner because of the nature of sin as an offence against a Person of infinite dignity.[18]

On the other hand, to re-frame the question as if it was merely about the extent of the atonement (as opposed to its intent) is to ask a slightly different question: 'what did Christ do?' as opposed to 'what did God intend?' Did Christ pay for the sins of those who are not elect of God and will end up in hell? Did he die for those not in the book of life, those said to be destined for a bad end (2 Corinthians 4:3, 1 Peter 2:8, 2 Peter 2:12, Jude 4, and Revelation 17:8)? That, of course, is a legitimate enquiry but it is not the way Calvinists themselves usually choose to define this question. Neither the final Canons of Dort nor the Westminster Confession (commonly reckoned to be the most authoritative statements of the Calvinist position) make formal statements on the question as stated in this way.[19] Extent and intent must be held together.

Dividing intent from extent can open up the theoretical possibility (attractive to some) of being a Calvinist on some points

---

[16] Not that there is anything inherently unsound about commercial language, since the New Testament uses the vocabulary of redemption (ἀπολύτρωσις in, for example, Ephesians 1:7 literally means 'buying back') and also of purchase (e.g. the verb ἀγοράζω in 1 Corinthians 6:20, 7:23 and 2 Peter 2:1) to describe the work of Christ.

[17] See Hodge, *Systematic Theology*, 2: p 544; R.L. Reymond, *A New Systematic Theology of the Christian Faith* (Nashville: Thomas Nelson, 1998), pp 672-673.

[18] Boettner, *The Reformed Doctrine*, pp 151-152.

[19] Cf. W. Cunningham, *Historical Theology* (Edinburgh: Banner of Truth, 1960), 2: p 326. On p 334, Cunningham agrees with Berkhof and the others listed in footnote 2 above that the question '*must* turn upon the question of the *purpose, design,* or *intention* of God.'

while demurring on limited atonement. Yet as soon as one considers Christ's accomplishment apart from God's design, further problems can emerge. What are sometimes called Amyraldian or 'four point Calvinist' solutions (we will examine the terminology later) imply a divergence between the Father's intention, the Son's execution, and the Spirit's application of the plan of salvation: God elects a limited number; Jesus dies for everyone; the Spirit applies the work of redemption to the elect alone.[20] This retains a Calvinist monergism (i.e. the Arminian 'free will' argument is not used to explain why all are not saved) but at the expense of agreement within the Godhead. For instance, J.C. Ryle says: 'In the work of the Father in election, and of the Spirit in conversion, I see limitation in the Bible most clearly. But in the work of Christ in atonement I see no limitation.'[21]

Paul Helm calls this conflict at the heart of the godhead 'the most fundamental theological criticism of Amyraldianism.'[22] It would seem to be inconsistent not only logically but more importantly *with scripture*. The Son who prayed to the Father 'not my will, but yours, be done' (Luke 22:42) also 'does nothing of his own accord' (John 5:19-24), while the Spirit will not act on his own authority, but in line with what Jesus has said (John 16:7-15). All three work in harmony as one. We cannot escape from this difficulty simply by imagining that the Trinity can all agree that there will be this discrepancy between their works (or that all three persons have determined a dual aspect of the atonement somehow). That might work logically, but is it attested by any text?

---

[20] See the comments of Armstrong on Amyraut's distinctive doctrine of the Trinity in Armstrong, *Calvinism and the Amyraut Heresy*, pp 172-177.

[21] *Expository Thoughts on John*, 1: p 62. Boettner, *The Reformed Doctrine*, p 156 also accuses *Arminians* of destroying the harmony of the Trinity. H. Bavinck, *Reformed Dogmatics: Sin and Salvation in Christ* (Grand Rapids: Baker, 2009), p 469. Van Genderen and Velema, *Concise Reformed Dogmatics*, p 528. This response to doctrines of unlimited atonement goes back at least to the ninth century with Gottschalk of Orbais; see his *On Predestination*, 5 in V. Genke and F.X. Gumerlock, *Gottschalk and A Medieval Predestination Controversy: Texts Translated from the Latin* (Milwaukee: Marquette University Press, 2010).

[22] See his review of another Amyraldian book in *Evangelicals Now* (2004) available online at http://www.e-n.org.uk/2749-Amyraut-affirmed-or-Owenism-a-caricature-of-Calvinism'.htm. See also John Frame's review of Armstrong's book in *Westminster Theological Journal* 34:2 (May 1972), p 191.

Whether we consider the eternal intent, historical extent, or historical and eternal effects of the atonement, in the end, however, we will bump up against the same doctrinal issues and exegetical puzzles. Similarly, although labels do matter in public debate because they can shape the preconceptions of the uncommitted, ultimately the same passages of scripture will come up for consideration and the same underlying questions will need to be addressed whatever we call this doctrine. Many advocates prefer the name 'particular redemption.' Some call it definite or efficacious atonement, as opposed to indefinite or universal atonement. The name 'unconditional atonement' may have some merit, since it emphasises that Christ even gives us the faith we need to appropriate salvation which is based on unconditional election, and the opposite 'conditional atonement' makes it clear that something extra is needed from that perspective. I have toyed with the term 'personal intentional effective atonement' myself because it is descriptive and shows what the alternative is (i.e. impersonal, random, and ineffective). It is not, however, very snappy (though it does spell PIE!) and it should really have a word like ecclesial in there too, because the Bible presents the cross not just as personal, 'for me', but as focused on the church, 'for us.' This wrecks the acronym, of course, which just goes to show that doctrines are like people: it is not easy to give them nicknames without stealing something of their complexity.

This doctrine did not go by the name 'limited atonement' in the sixteenth, seventeenth, or eighteenth centuries. Atonement is a sixteenth century word and appears in the 1611 King James Version of the Bible, but the doctrine we are discussing usually went by the name of redemption rather than atonement. The L word was sometimes used in reference to this, as in a book against Arminianism by William Troughton called *Scripture Redemption, Restrayned and Limited, or, An Antidote against Universal Redemption* (1652). Troughton also calls his Anti-Arminian doctrine 'peculiar redemption.' The earliest reference to 'limited atonement' to describe this doctrine, that I have found, is in an American book from 1814.[23] It seems to become the popular name only from the

---

[23]   J.F. Schermerhorn and S.J. Mills, *A Correct View of That Part of the United States which Lies West of the Allegany Mountains: with regard to Religion and Morals* (Hartford, 1814), p 6.

1820s, however, perhaps because of its use in a magical attempt to reconcile Calvinists and Arminians on the issue, conjured up by Edward Dorr Griffin in 1819.[24]

The name became famous, of course, and assured a place in Christian pedagogy, when some clever soul thought up the acronym TULIP to describe the five points of Calvinism as discussed at the Synod of Dort. The names of all five (total depravity, limited atonement, unconditional election, irresistible grace, and preservation of the saints) were given the necessary starting initials by Philip Schaff in 1892.[25] However, the first use of the flowery acronym itself (which required a rearrangement in the order of the petals) was probably in the twentieth century.[26] In the seventeenth century, as now, tulips were popular in the Netherlands, so it is not an inappropriate flower to be associated with a Dutch Synod.[27] The acronym is not entirely helpful, however, as it requires careful explanation of terms like 'total' and 'irresistible' if it is accurately to reflect Reformed thought. It often leads to misunderstanding such that some Reformed thinkers wish to uproot TULIP altogether.[28]

The main drawback with continuing to use the name 'limited atonement' for the doctrine is that, as Don Carson says, it is 'objectively misleading' since 'every view of the atonement "limits" it

---

[24] Griffin, Dorr, *An Humble Attempt to Reconcile the Differences of Christians Respecting the Extent of the Atonement* (New York, 1819).

[25] P. Schaff, *History of the Christian Church* (New York, 1892), 8: p 815.

[26] See the appendix in K.J. Stewart, *Ten Myths about Calvinism: Recovering the Breadth of the Reformed Tradition* (Downers Grove: IVP, 2011), pp 291-292 for mention of its use around 1905.

[27] William Aglionby, *The Present State of the United Provinces of the Low-Countries* (London, 1669), p 283 speaks of a time when 'the fancy for tulips did reign over all the Low Countries.' Indeed, though overstated, Charles Mackay's *Extraordinary Popular Delusions and the Madness of Crowds* (1841) chronicles the famous Dutch 'tulip mania' of 1637 when the price of a single bulb bubbled to extraordinary heights. Cf. Jan Brueghel the Younger's painting *Satire on Tulip Mania* (1640).

[28] See R.A. Muller, 'Was Calvin a Calvinist? Or, Did Calvin (or Anyone Else in the Early Modern Era) Plant the "TULIP"?' available at http://www.calvin.edu/meeter/lectures/Richard%20Muller%20-%20Was%20Calvin%20a%20Calvinist.pdf.
Timothy George, *Amazing Grace: God's Pursuit, Our Response* (Wheaton: Crossway, 2011), p 84 has suggested the alternative botanical acronym ROSES, which stands for Radical depravity, Overcoming grace, Sovereign election, Eternal life, and Singular redemption!

in some way, save for the view of the unqualified universalist.'[29] This can be seen in the writings of, for instance, Arminian scholar Ben Witherington III, who writes that

> The Reformation inclination to say the atonement is limited was correct, but... Christ came to die for sinners, not the elect. Indeed... God desires all persons to be saved... and Christ gave himself as a ransom for all sinners. This means that it must be human beings in their response to God in Christ, not God through some process of choosing individuals, who limit the atonement.[30]

So both Calvinists and Arminians believe in 'limited atonement' in some sense! The question is, what is it that imposes the limitation? Is it God in his wise design, or is it humanity in its free choice? Charles Hodge was right to respond to statements like this one from Witherington by saying that because of its focus on human free will, it is the *Arminian* doctrine which 'is the limited and meagre scheme; whereas the orthodox doctrine is catholic and comprehensive.'[31] Nevertheless, the most common and immediately recognisable designation for this doctrine remains 'limited atonement,' though I will use it alongside other names here.[32]

---

[29]   Carson, *The Difficult Doctrine*, (Leicester: IVP, 2000), p 84.

[30]   B. Witherington, *The Problem with Evangelical Theology: Testing the Exegetical Foundations of Calvinism, Dispensationalism and Wesleyanism* (Waco: Baylor University Press, 2005), p 88.

[31]   Hodge, *Systematic Theology*, 2: p 562.

[32]   I will also use the words 'Calvinist' and 'Calvinism' alongside 'Reformed' for the same sorts of reasons, though again, as Richard Muller has rightly warned, we must be aware of the technical difficulties of using this shorthand. 'Calvinian' and 'Calvinism' have been used in English, however, as understandable terms to describe a school of Protestant thought distinct from Lutheranism since the 1560s. See, for example, the marginal note in Stanislaw Hozjusz, *Of the Express Worde of God* (1567), p69b and Ninian Winzet, *The Buke of Fourscoir-thre Questions Tueching Doctrine, Ordour, and Maneris* (1563) which uses the word 'Calvinian' even within Calvin's own lifetime.

2.   EXEGETICAL ARGUMENTS

2.1.   *Logical arguments for limited atonement*

R.T. Kendall wonders 'how many Christians would ever come to the view of limited atonement merely by reading the Bible!'[1] The clear implication of such a statement is that it is 'a textless doctrine',[2] which would indeed be a serious flaw.

It is true that logical arguments have been used to support the case. It will help to get a feel for these first before we examine the scriptures, *not because logic is more important than the Bible*, but because some exegetical details become more important when we appreciate the logical case they are intended to support. One such logical argument is this: 'if Jesus died for all the sins even of the non-elect, then is it not unjust for God to demand double payment for the same sins, by sending those people to hell?'[3] A similar argument from double payment or 'dual atonement' is used by *non*-Reformed writers in other contexts, such as in the argument against capital

Logical Argumen

---

[1]   R.T. Kendall, *Calvin and English Calvinism*, viii.

[2]   The explicit accusation of Knox, 'Some Aspects', p 263. Though as one scholar says, 'It is unnecessarily reductionistic to suggest that a doctrine is biblical only if a proof text can be adduced.' Mark D. Thompson, 'The Divine Investment in Truth: *Toward a Theological Account of Biblical Inerrancy*' in J.K. Hoffmeier and D.R. Magary (eds.), *Do Historical Matters Matter to Faith?* (Wheaton: Crossway, 2012), p 75.

[3]   C.H. Spurgeon (as quoted in Boettner, *The Reformed Doctrine*, p 155) used this argument. See also W.A. Elwell, 'Atonement, Extent of the' in Elwell, *Evangelical Dictionary of Theology*, p 98 as well as Grudem, *Systematic Theology*, p 595 and Hodge, *Systematic Theology*, 2: p 557. I do not think Isaiah 40:2, 'she has received from the hand of the LORD double for all her sins' means that God *does* punish people twice. The Hebrew word for 'double' here (כִּפְלַיִם *kiphlayim*), meant in context as a comfort after all, actually means Israel has received the full amount of punishment; if it was, so to speak, folded over (*doubled* over) onto her sins, it would match them exactly. Where Hebrew wants to convey the idea of a punishment that is 'twice as much', it uses a different word (as in Exodus 22:4, 7, 9). See J.A. Motyer, *The Prophecy of Isaiah* (Leicester: IVP, 1993), p 299 and G. Von Rad, ' כִּפְלַיִם in Jes. 40.2 = "Äquivalent"?' in *Zeitschrift für die Alttestamentliche Wissenschaft* 79 (1967), pp 80-82 who also suggests a parallel with Jeremiah 16:18.

punishment, even though many disavow its use in favour of limited atonement.[4]

Other Reformed theologians ask how God can punish the reprobate in hell if he is unchangeable and supposedly loves everyone the same. Surely we have to either jettison his immutability or say he only loves the elect in a saving way?[5] John Owen also put the general logical case compellingly like this: was Christ punished for

a) all the sins of all men
b) some sins of all men, or
c) all the sins of some men?

If the first, then all are saved! If lack of faith is adduced as a reason for denying this universal salvation to some then Owen asks why, if Christ died for *all* the sins of even the reprobate, does this not include their unbelief which is, surely, one such sin? If unbelief is not a sin then why should they be punished for it? If the second option is correct, then we all still have some sins to answer for, and so are not saved by the cross at all. This leaves only the third option, which is that Christ was punished for all the sins of the elect, who are truly and effectively saved by it.[6]

---

4   On the use of the 'dual atonement is wrong' idea (that Christ atoned for all and therefore that capital punishment is no longer justifiable), see C.D. Marshall, *Beyond Retribution: A New Testament Vision for Justice, Crime, and Punishment* (Cambridge: Eerdmans, 2001), p 222. See also the theoretical invocation of limited atonement in favour of capital punishment in D.W.S. Belousek, *Atonement, Justice, and Peace: The Message of the Cross and the Mission of the Church* (Cambridge: Eerdmans, 2012), p 500.

5   Jonathan Moore, 'James Ussher's Influence on the Synod of Dordt,' in Aza Goudriaan and Fred van Lieburg (eds.), *Revisiting the Synod of Dordt* (Leiden: Brill, 2011), p 167.

6   J. Owen, *The Works of John Owen* (Edinburgh: Banner of Truth, 1967), 10: pp 173-174 and 249. Although John Owen's very helpful book *The Death of Death* (1647) is often considered *the* book on limited atonement, his voice is just one of a number of Reformed voices in this debate and not everyone within that tradition would agree with Owen on every detail of how he defends this doctrine. Dissenting from Owen on some issues does not (of necessity) put one outside the pale of Reformed orthodoxy! I say this here particularly because some people seem to (erroneously) imagine that because my doctoral research is on Owen I must agree with and want to push his point of view as the exclusive acme of excellence. That being said, his point here is very well made.

While such questions have their place and surely deserve an answer, advocates of effective personal atonement are keen to stress that they arrive at their doctrinal conclusions on the basis of serious exegetical study not simply through logic. Logic has its place, and is a biblical tool for discovering truth. We need only mention the fact that the logical connective 'therefore' occurs about 800 times in the Bible to see this very clearly! A study of how logic is used in scripture, not least in intra-biblical interpretation (e.g. Hebrews 1:1-2:4 or Matthew 22:45) is extremely rewarding.[7] A recent philosophical paper argued that the existence of logic is actually a powerful argument for the existence of God,[8] and John Piper makes a great point when he writes that, 'Jesus assumes that human beings use logic, and he holds them accountable to use their logic well.'[9] So it is clear, as John Frame has argued, that 'It is Scripture that warrants our use of logic, not the other way around.'[10]

This being said, Reformed theologians would emphatically reject the idea that they squeeze God into a pre-existing, philosophically determined framework. Grudem perhaps plays into opponents' hands when he writes that 'limited atonement is necessarily part of a Reformed viewpoint *because it logically follows* from the overall sovereignty of God in the entire work of redemption.'[11] It may well be logically consistent to believe in limited atonement, given the other four points of Calvinism, but it can only truly lay claim to be 'part of a Reformed viewpoint' if it is, first and foremost, consistent with the word of God.[12]

---

[7] See Jesus' use of logical connections such as analogy (e.g. Luke 11:13), *reductio ad absurdum* (e.g. Matthew 12:26), the excluded middle (e.g. Matthew 12:30), *a fortiori* argument (e.g. Matthew 12:1-8), implication (e.g. Matthew 12:28), and the law of non-contradiction (e.g. Luke 6:39).

[8] Or, 'the laws of logic are metaphysically dependent on the existence of God.' See J.N. Anderson and G. Welty, 'The Lord of Non-Contradiction: An Argument for God from Logic' in *Philosophia Christi* 13:2 (2011), pp 321-338.

[9] John Piper, 'The Pastor as Scholar' in J. Piper and D.A. Carson, *The Pastor as Scholar and the Scholar as Pastor* edited by O. Strachan and D. Mathis (Wheaton: Crossway, 2011), p 55 (particularly focusing on Luke 12:54-57).

[10] John Frame, *The Doctrine of the Knowledge of God* (Phillipsburg, NJ: P&R, 1987), p 243.

[11] Grudem, *Systematic Theology*, p 596 n34 (my emphasis).

[12] Hodge, *Systematic Theology*, 2: pp 546f also appears to make too much of logic before getting to scripture.

The Bible itself encourages us to ask careful questions of its sometimes seemingly incompatible statements. The Lord wants us to wrestle with them and meditate on them, making judicious distinctions so as to understand them correctly within the whole counsel of God. As David Scaer rightly points out, 'The conflict concerning the nature and extent of the atonement arose in Christian theology because of attempts to reconcile rationally apparently conflicting statements in the Holy scriptures on the atonement and election.'[13] Other conflicts have arisen because of the need to wrestle with such apparent difficulties. For example, 'the LORD our God, the LORD is one' (Deuteronomy 6:4) seems to be at odds with the New Testament's ascription of divinity to both the Father and Jesus (e.g. John 1:1, Romans 9:5, Titus 2:13, 2 Peter 1:1-2). Reflecting on this led the church to develop the doctrine of the Trinity. Likewise, Ezekiel 18:32 says, 'I have no pleasure in the death of the one who is dying, declares the Lord GOD,' and yet in 1 Samuel 2:25, God specifically says it *is* his pleasure (the very same word, חָפֵץ *chaphetz*) to kill certain people. Are those Jesus died for his friends (John 15:13) or his enemies (Romans 5:10)? Shall we read these verses superficially and posit a straightforward contradiction in God's statements, accusing him of inconsistency? Or do we work hard to understand the specific meaning of each verse in its context and attempt so to interpret scripture that one part is not made 'repugnant to another' (as the *Thirty-nine Articles* encourage us)?[14]

We should not hurriedly embrace any opinion which a few isolated verses of scripture seem at first sight to give countenance to. We must listen humbly to the word, carefully and prayerfully testing our initial impressions against the sweep of the whole. Otherwise we risk coming to hasty conclusions which greater biblical knowledge and more mature reflection may prove to have been faulty. Hence it is often when meditating on apparently 'universal' texts like 1 John 2:2, 1 Timothy 2:4-6, or 2 Peter 2:1 that people start to ponder these issues more deeply. The question of the extent or intent of the atonement arises directly out of serious Bible study when scripture itself is used to interpret scripture.

---

[13] D. Scaer, 'The Nature and Extent of the Atonement in Lutheran Theology,' in *Bulletin of the Evangelical Theological Society* 10.4 (1967), p 179.

[14] Article 20.

Those who hold to limited atonement therefore believe that it makes more sense of the Bible's witness as a whole. They would suggest that the supposedly 'straightforward' yet atomistic reading of the universal texts creates more problems *biblically* than it solves. If we are to reject the doctrine of definite atonement *simply* because 1 John 2:2 says Jesus was the propitiation 'not for our sins only, but also for the sins of the whole world,' then must we not also reject the Protestant doctrine of justification *simply* because James 2:24 says 'a person is justified by works and not by faith alone'?

The desire for a tidy system of theology with neat resolutions to every difficulty is understandable, even if it may not be entirely achievable. On the other hand, it would be shallow simply to lay seemingly contradictory statements from the Bible side by side and not attempt to understand how they cohere. It would be especially irresponsible to do this if the Bible itself gives us clues as to how they might be harmonised. To take refuge in paradox or 'mystery' too quickly and easily is to miss out on the fullness of the word, which God has given us for our delight and obedience. We are meant to chew on these things, not wolf them down whole without further thought.

2.2. *Exegetical arguments for limited atonement*

So what we really need is to account for the richness of the witness of scripture, first and foremost. We will, therefore, consider some of the exegetical arguments used on both sides of the argument. Rather than attempt a whole 'biblical theology of limited atonement,' which would be possible but too detailed, I will instead present the four main biblical arguments which, together, are used to support particular redemption.

2.2.1. *For us and for our salvation*

First, Reformed exegetes usually point to those texts which affirm that Christ died with a particular reference to a limited group of people. At the very start of the Gospels we hear that Jesus has come to 'save *his people* from their sins' (Matthew 1:21).[15] John the Baptist's father rejoices that God 'has visited and achieved redemption *for his people*' (Luke 1:68). Jesus himself tells his disciples that 'the Son of Man did not come to be served but to serve, and to give his life as a ransom for *many*' (Matthew 20:28 and parallels).[16] This, of course, is what he repeats when he institutes the Lord's Supper: 'this is my blood of the covenant, which is poured out for *many* for the forgiveness of sins' (Matthew 26:28).

So he died for those given to him by the Father. It is difficult to read John 6:38-39 in a way which suggests that the Father sent Jesus to die for people who will remain lost. Rather, Jesus was sent by the Father to save a particular group of people and to make sure they are indeed saved on the last day: 'that nothing of all he has given to me should be lost, but rather, I will raise it up on the last day.' The Father also wills them to believe (6:40), which reinforces the idea of an intentional design to save a particular group (decided on beforehand and 'given' to Jesus).

More explicitly, the Lord Jesus himself said that he came to die for his sheep, wherever they are scattered. He said, 'I am the good shepherd. The good shepherd lays down his life for the sheep' (John 10:11, 15). He has other sheep elsewhere (John 10:16), presumably the elect amongst the Gentiles or the as yet unborn. But there are others

---

[15] D.A. Carson, *Matthew* (Grand Rapids: Zondervan, 1995), 1: p 76 helpfully draws out how the meaning of 'his people' is widened as the Gospel progresses, so that it comes to mean 'Messiah's people' (including both a Jewish 'godly remnant' and believing Gentiles). In the same vein, Thomas Aquinas quotes Remigius on this verse as saying, 'He saves indeed not the unbelieving, but his people; that is, he saves those that believe on him.' Peter Chrysologus adds that he saves *his people*, 'not any other man's people.' Thomas Aquinas, *Catena Aurea: Commentary on the Four Gospels* (Oxford: John Henry Parker, 1841), 1: p 51.

[16] Some commentators take 'many' here as equivalent to 'all,' or as an undefined mass in contrast to the Son of Man, but the absence of the definite article is against this. See L. Morris, *The Gospel According to Matthew* (Leicester: Apollos, 1992), p 512 n47. Cf. Paul's desire to seek not what was advantageous to himself but what was advantageous for *the many* (τῶν πολλῶν) that they may be saved (1 Corinthians 10:33).

who are simply not part of his flock and do not listen to his voice.[17] He does not give them eternal life, but is focused only on those who have been given to him by the Father (John 10:26-29). He also tells his disciples in John 15:13-16 that, 'No-one has greater love than this, that he lays down his life for his friends. You are my friends if you do what I command you... It was not you who chose me, but I chose you and appointed you that you should go and bear fruit.' So it seems that John presents us with a Messiah who comes to die for his chosen friends, the ones given to him by the Father in eternity. Indeed, John 17:9 shows that those given to Jesus by the Father are a limited group, and explicitly said *not* to be 'the world' (κόσμος, *kosmos*).

In Acts 20:28 Paul exhorts the Ephesian elders to pay attention to the flock and 'to shepherd (or pastor) the church of God, which he acquired with his own blood' (or 'the blood of his own,' that is his own Son, Jesus). Again we see that the blood of Christ specifically purchased the sheep, the church.[18] The same picture is presented in Ephesians 5:25-27 where Paul writes, 'Husbands, love your wives, as Christ loved the church and *gave himself up for her*, that he might sanctify *her*, having cleansed *her* by the washing of water with the word, so that he might present *the church* to himself in splendor, without spot or wrinkle or any such thing, that *she* might be holy and blameless.' In the context of marriage, a very definite and particular love is on view here, one that is focused on the bride, the church. There is also an inseparable unity between Christ's death for the church and his sanctification and cleansing of it. As Edwin Palmer put it, 'Those for whom he died he also sanctifies and cleanses.'[19]

Famously, the Apostle elsewhere speaks of 'the Son of God who loved me and gave himself up for me' (Galatians 2:20). He thus includes himself in the church, part of the bride of Christ. The concept is again nuanced so that it is possible to speak of Christ dying

---

[17] C.K. Barrett, *The Gospel According to St John: An Introduction with Commentary and Notes on the Greek Text* (London: SPCK, 1955), p 312 calls this a 'predestined distinction' contrasting unbelieving Jews with believers amongst both Jews and Gentiles.

[18] There is no escaping the 'commercial' nature of the language here, as D.G. Peterson, *The Acts of the Apostles* (Nottingham: Apollos, 2009), p 570 makes clear.

[19] E.H. Palmer, *The Five Points of Calvinism* (Grand Rapids: Baker, 2010), p 52.

not just for his church or for 'me' but also for his family. So in 1 Corinthians 8:11 he mentions 'the brother for whom Christ died.' Again, in Romans 14:15, he speaks of 'the one for whom Christ died,' who in that same verse is called 'your brother.' Christ gave himself up to death for me, my Christian brothers and sisters, and for his church. So it is unsurprising that when Paul refers to Christ and the church in other places he speaks of him giving himself for 'us', his saved people (Titus 2:14 cf. 'us' in 2:8 and 3:5).[20] The purpose of the atonement in Titus 2:14 is 'that he might purify for himself *a specially-chosen people*' (λαὸν περιούσιον, *laon periousion*), a phrase taken up from Deuteronomy 7:6, 14:2, and 26:18 referring to those purified by the cross as like 'property owned as a rich and distinctive possession.'[21] They are 'God's elect,' for whom he died and is interceding (Romans 8:32-34).[22]

This picture is preserved all the way to the end of the Bible. In Revelation 5 a new song is sung to the Lamb who was slain: 'Worthy are you to take the book and to open its seals, because you were slain, and by your blood you ransomed for God people *out of* every tribe and language and people and nation, and you have made them a kingdom and priests for our God, and they shall reign on the earth' (Revelation 5:9-10). Although the 'eternal gospel' is proclaimed to every nation, tribe, language, and people (Revelation 14:6), his blood

---

[20] G.W. Knight, *The Pastoral Epistles: A Commentary on the Greek Text* (Cambridge: Eerdmans, 1992), p 327 suggests an echo in Titus 2:14 of Jesus' words in Matthew 20:28 where he gave himself (the same verb, δίδωμι, is used) for *many*. The *many* is now interpreted as those who accept Christ as their God and Saviour (verse 13), i.e. 'us.'

[21] See B. Friberg, T. Friberg, and N. Miller, *Analytical Lexicon of the Greek New Testament* (Grand Rapids: Baker, 2000) on περιούσιον. Cf. J.E. Louw and E.A. Nida, *Greek-English Lexicon of the New Testament Based on Semantic Domains: Second Edition* (United Bible Societies, 1989) which gives the sense of 'people who belong to him alone.'

[22] T.R. Schreiner, *Romans* (Grand Rapids: Baker, 1998), p 463 is absolutely right to insist that 'This intercession should not be separated from his death on behalf of his people'; a point which will become more important when we consider the views of R.T. Kendall.

only redeems some *out of* (ἐκ, *ek*) this group.[23] It does not indicate that every tribe and nation as a whole was redeemed, for it is clear that only some chosen from among the peoples are made 'a kingdom and priests for our God.' Yet this chorus in heaven considers those who are Christ's kingdom and those who shall reign over the new creation to be the same group as those who have been redeemed by the blood of the lamb (as in Revelation 1:5-6). As Greg Beale says, 'This is not a redemption of all peoples without exception, but of all without distinction (people *from* all races).'[24]

Space precludes a more detailed look at every passage in the Bible which has been seen as indicating particular redemption. Yet the brevity of these few paragraphs may be deceiving: the biblical evidence for a focused, personal, intentional design in the work of Christ is profuse, diverse, and deeply embedded in the earliest proclamation of the gospel. We would do well to look up and meditate on each of these passages.

The Roman Catholic position attempts to use Romans 8:32 as a proof text for universal atonement. In 1965 at the Second Vatican Council, it was affirmed that,

> by His incarnation the Son of God has united Himself in some fashion with every man... As an innocent lamb He merited for us life by the free shedding of His own blood. In Him God reconciled us to Himself and among ourselves; from bondage to the devil and sin He delivered us, so that each one of us can say with the Apostle: The Son of God "loved me and gave Himself up for me" (Galatians 2:20). By suffering for us He not only provided us with an example for

---

[23] Similarly, in Genesis 6:19-21 Noah takes into the ark 'from every living thing' and 'from every sort of food' (מִכָּל), or with A. Pietersma and B.G. Wright, *A New English Translation of the Septuagint* (Oxford: Oxford University Press, 2007), translating ἀπὸ πάντων, 'some of all'. In the LXX, the Greek preposition used alongside the word for 'all' is different (ἀπὸ not ἐκ), but 'out of' would be an equally good translation of the מ in מִכָּל, as in Genesis 2:9 for example, where trees come out of (מִן / ἐκ) the ground. So the idea is essentially the same as in Revelation 5:9. The ark is designed only to save some chosen out of the whole.

[24] G.K. Beale, *The Book of Revelation: A Commentary on the Greek Text* (Cambridge: Eerdmans, 1999), p 359. G. Osborne, *Revelation* (Grand Rapids: Baker, 2002), p 260 suggests an allusion here to Exodus 19:5 where God says to Israel, 'out of all the nations you will be my treasured possession.'

our imitation, He blazed a trail, and if we follow it, life and death are made holy and take on a new meaning... **All this holds true not only for Christians**, but for all men of good will in whose hearts grace works in an unseen way. For, **since Christ died for all men**, (Romans 8:32) and since the ultimate vocation of man is in fact one, and divine, we ought to believe that the Holy Spirit in a manner known only to God offers to every man the possibility of being associated with this paschal mystery.[25]

Romans 8:32 is, however, a key text for *particular* atonement since it seems to affirm that those for whom Christ died will also be given every spiritual blessing: 'He who did not even spare his own Son but gave him up for us all, how will he not also, along with him, graciously give to us all things?' The emphasis here is not just on the generous character of God but also on the identity of the recipients: 'us' in the context of Romans 8 equals Spirit-indwelt, suffering, children of God in Christ, who in the very next verse (Romans 8:33) are called 'God's elect'.[26] So, the argument goes, Christ's death for someone and their receiving of the benefits of his passion are inextricably linked. If Christ died for everyone without exception, even the non-elect, then according to the logic of this verse everyone without exception would qualify for and receive 'all things' from God (which presumably includes glorification, verse 30).

So, discounting the possibility of universal salvation, definite atonement appears to be the underlying assumption of Romans 8:32.[27] It also appears to underlie Romans 5:10 – 'if, being enemies, we were reconciled to God through the death of his Son, *how much*

---

[25] *Pastoral Constitution on the Church in the Modern World: Gaudium et Spes* (1965), chapter 1, number 22.

[26] In Romans 4:25, 'he was handed over for *our* trespasses' and Romans 5:8, 'Christ died for *us*' the most natural referent is, again, *believers* rather than every single person who ever has lived or shall live, especially since the verse immediately following (in both cases) can *only* be referring to believers (cf. also Romans 4:24).

[27] This is often brought out by advocates of particular redemption, and dates back at least as far as Gottschalk of Orbais in the ninth century. See his *Answers to Various Questions*, 6 in Genke and Gumerlock, *Gottschalk*, p 105. It is clear too that Augustine, e.g. in *On Reprimand and Grace* 7:15 considers Romans 8:32 to be about the elect, for whom Christ suffered and shed his blood, who also persevere in faith to the end.

more, being reconciled, we shall be saved by his life.'[28] If his death was truly 'for us' and reconciled us, then we can safely assume we shall be saved from God's coming wrath. If we are not saved on the Last Day, then Christ did not die for us.

Furthermore, 2 Corinthians 5:14 teaches that those 'for whom Christ died' have died with him (however we understand 'all' in that verse). When this is placed alongside Paul's emphasis in Romans 6:5-8 that 'if we died with Christ, we believe that we shall also live with him' (6:8) it strongly suggests that Paul's underlying assumption must be either definite atonement or universal salvation.[29] As Sinclair Ferguson puts it, emphasizing the Pauline idea of union with Christ, 'If Christ died for us, we died in Christ.'[30] Similarly, Paul Barnett speaks of 'the "all" for whom Christ died, who also have "died" in him,' concluding that 'The "all" who have died "in Christ" are not coextensive with the "all" who sin and die "in Adam." The end of death [is]... only for those who are "in" Jesus Christ.'[31]

These are the kind of texts which lead those who favour limited atonement to consider the unlimited atonement position as more than potentially universalist. Paul's argument in Romans 8:32 is that God will not withhold anything from those for whom Christ died. If he died for all without exception then surely all without exception will be eternally saved?

Those who favour the universal atonement position answer these opening arguments by pointing out that although scripture does say Christ died for his sheep, it does not follow logically that he

---

[28] C.E.B. Cranfield, *Romans: A Shorter Commentary* (Edinburgh: T&T Clark, 1985), pp 208-209 supports this by also linking Romans 8:32 with 5:9-10 and suggesting that by 'all things' in 8:32 'is probably meant the fullness of salvation (compare 5:10) or else "all that is necessary for our salvation".' So if Christ died for us, we will also obtain everything necessary for our salvation (e.g. faith, perseverance etc).

[29] Owen, *Works*, 10: pp 350-352. Cf. Jeffery, Ovey, and Sach, *Pierced for our Transgressions*, pp 272-273.

[30] S.B. Ferguson, 'Preaching the Atonement,' in Hill and James, *The Glory of the Atonement*, p 434.

[31] P. Barnett, *The Second Epistle to the Corinthians* (Cambridge: Eerdmans, 1997), p 290 (on 2 Corinthians 5:14).

did so *only* for them.[32] This logical observation is of course perfectly true;[33] but the universal atonement case does not logically follow from the observation. Paul says the Son of God loved him and gave himself for him (Galatians 2:20); that does not logically exclude the idea that he gave himself for others apart from Paul, of course, yet it does not prove he died for everyone indiscriminately either. If one is going to apply Aristotelian logic in an attempt to refute limited atonement, it should at least be applied carefully and consistently.

Most Calvinist theologians would argue that limited atonement makes better sense of these texts. They can plausibly claim, for example, that the more universal statements are about universal sufficiency or invitation (as we shall see). It is true that alongside the positive statements (e.g. Christ died for his sheep), the negative side (he did *not* die for the goats) is not always stated explicitly. It is fairly clear in Revelation 5:9 that some are excluded, when Jesus is praised because 'by your blood you ransomed for God people *out of* every tribe and language and people and nation, and you have made *them* a kingdom and priests for our God, and *they* shall reign on the earth.' But it is true that it is not always so clear.

All the same, Calvinists might argue that the unlimited position cannot really explain 'why limited or definite language should ever have been employed, if there was really no limitation in the object or destination of the atonement.'[34] This is difficult to answer, especially since universalising them seems to cut the cord of assurance and joy given by the particularised statements. Consider this: if a girl tells a boy she loves him (ahhh!), this may have a very positive effect on him; but if she then immediately proceeds to say she loves everyone in the room, and embraces them all equally, this may encourage him far less and his hopes and expectations are dashed. So it is, we might argue, if verses which speak of personal/ecclesial effective atonement are undermined by a doctrine of universal atonement.

---

[32] T.L. Miethe, 'The Universal Power of the Atonement,' in C. Pinnock (ed.), *The Grace of God, The Will of Man: A Case for Arminianism* (Grand Rapids: Zondervan, 1989), p 73.

[33] As Reymond, *A New Systematic Theology*, pp 673-674 is also quick to acknowledge.

[34] Cunningham, *Historical Theology*, 2: p 340.

So we ponder the nature of the marriage illustration in Ephesians 5. Christ gave himself up for the church, his bride. What happens if we tamper with this and say that Christ somehow gave himself up for others (i.e. those who do not and will never believe in him)? Does it not subvert the very picture of exclusive, monogamous marriage which parallels Christ's loving sacrifice? This would unwittingly encourage something like polygamy, which is clearly not endorsed![35] It is certainly noteworthy that husbands are not told to love their wives 'as God loved the world,' but as Christ loved the church and gave himself up for her. It is a particular love, not a general philanthropy, and the exhortation loses its force if Christ gave himself up for all without exception.

However, the case for limited atonement does not in any case rest *solely* on the observation that scripture says (for example) 'Christ died for his Church.' It requires the other arguments below (i.e. that atonement is efficacious and also bestows the conditions of salvation) to hold true as well.[36] So it is not claimed that these verses alone prove the case.

On the other hand, it is claimed that definite atonement makes better sense of the passages in which phrases such as 'Christ laid down his life for his friends' occur. So it affirms through contextual exegesis that Jesus did not die for the non-elect (for if he had, the argument of Romans 8:32 would not make sense); he did not die for strangers, wolves, thieves, robbers and those outside his flock as he did for his sheep (for that would make no sense in the narrative thought-world of John 10).[37] Indeed, in John 10:26 the Lord says that some do not believe because they are not of his flock (not, note, vice-versa),[38] so the difference is caused by something apart from and prior

---

[35]   See Reymond, *A New Systematic Theology*, p 674. Palmer, *The Five Points*, p 52.

[36]   Note that these arguments are used right next to each other in the same sentence in Packer, 'The Love of God', p 288.

[37]   A point made as far back as Gottschalk, *On Predestination*, 6: 'He himself says that the Son of God suffered only for the elect: *I lay down my life for the sheep* (John 10:15), that is, not – God forbid! – for another's goats and kids. But we should believe Christ, not – God forbid! – heretics, that the sheep of Christ, redeemed by Christ's blood, do not perish.' See also D.A. Carson, *The Gospel According to John*, p 387 on the peculiar intentionality of the cross as based on the mutual knowledge of the Father and Son.

[38]   Cf. Reymond, *A New Systematic Theology*, p 674.

to the human response of faith.[39] Whatever that is, it restricts the number of those who benefit from the laying down of the shepherd's life (10:15).

Arminius argued that 'the decree of Predestination prescribes nothing [sets no bounds] to the universality of the price paid for all by the death of Christ.'[40] That is not the picture we see in Ephesians, however. Just as the elect were chosen to be 'holy and blameless' (ἁγίους καὶ ἀμώμους, *hagious kai amomous*) before God (Ephesians 1:4), so Christ gave himself up to make his bride 'holy and blameless' (ἁγία καὶ ἄμωμος, *hagia kai amomos*, Ephesians 5:25-27). The same Greek words are used here.[41] The cross achieved what predestination planned. They have the same end and goal; our redemption through his blood is the temporal consequence of God's eternal choice of us, and the means by which he saves us and removes our blemishes. Eternal election works itself out by means of temporal atonement appropriated by faith alone, but it is election not just to faith but to sanctification and final salvation too.

There are other passages which link God's eternal will and intention to the coming of Christ 'for us and for our salvation.' Galatians 1:4 speaks of Christ 'who gave himself for our sins so that he might deliver us out of the present evil age, according to the will of our God and Father.' The cross achieved the costly deliverance which God's eternal will designed. 2 Timothy 1:9-10 also indicates that Paul thinks 'the appearance of our Saviour Christ Jesus' to 'abolish death' was directly related to God's purpose before the world began. There is a causal link between the plan of God and the coming of Christ, which is focused on the salvation and holy calling of 'us,' that is, the people of God. This eternal perspective which the Bible gives us explains the other references to Christ giving himself for his people, his sheep, his church, his bride.

---

[39] See Murray, 'The Atonement and the Free Offer', pp 74-76. Note verse 16 where others who have not yet believed are nevertheless termed sheep rather than wolves. They may be lost sheep, at present, but they are sheep.

[40] *The Writings of James Arminius* (Grand Rapids: Baker, 1956), 3: p 346.

[41] For some reason, the ESV translates 'blameless' (Ephesians 1:4) as 'without blemish' in Ephesians 5:27, though it is the same word in Greek. See also Colossians 1:22, Jude 24, and Revelation 14:5.

In the same way, according to the apostle Peter, certain people were designated 'elect exiles… according to the forethought of God the Father, by sanctification of the Spirit, for obedience and sprinkling with the blood of Jesus Christ' (1 Peter 1:1-2). The cross was designed to put this decree into effect, as Jesus was 'delivered up according to the determined purpose and forethought of God' (Peter again, in Acts 2:23).[42] Election and atonement are intimately linked and related. Christ came to die for the elect exiles that they might be 'sprinkled with his blood' in accordance with God's definite plan. Grudem is correct, but perhaps too restrained, when he concludes that, 'Even if they do not absolutely imply such a particularizing of redemption, [such] verses do at least seem to be most naturally interpreted in this way.'[43]

2.2.2. *Definite atonement*

The second line of biblical argument in favour of personal redemption is that scripture presents the atonement as actually achieving salvation for people. It reconciles the Father to us (as Article 2 of the *Thirty-nine Articles* strikingly puts it), rather than merely making salvation possible for all. In the Old Testament, in non-Messianic contexts, there are examples of 'substitutionary death' language, with particular beneficiaries in mind, who would be definitely saved. When, for example, David cries, 'If only I had died instead of you, O Absalom!' in 2 Samuel 18:33 he did not mean, 'I wish I could have died so there was a possibility that you might (if you want to) be saved.' He meant, 'If I died in your place, you would certainly be saved and live.' The same Hebrew preposition (תַּחַת *tachath*) is used here as in Genesis 22:13 when Abraham sacrifices a ram 'instead of' his son, who is, thereby, definitely freed.[44]

---

[42] For πρόγνωσις as meaning forethought or prearrangement and not just passively being aware of something in advance, see J.H. Thayer, *A Greek-English Lexicon of the New Testament* (1889).

[43] Grudem, *Systematic Theology*, p 600.

[44] Standard Hebrew and Old Testament dictionaries such as BDB, HALOT, and TWOT indicate that the word means 'instead of' or 'for the sake of.' I am not, of course, implying that David was to be a penal substitute to rescue Absalom from God's wrath (that's not what the story is about!).

Advocates of particular redemption would say that these Old Testament examples are illuminating for the New Testament language of dying in someone's place. Great David's greater Son, the Lord Jesus, actually does die for his rebellious children, not just to make their salvation possible. The Old Testament terminology lying behind this New Testament fulfilment implies that if someone 'dies for you' then you are truly released; your salvation is particular but also definite.[45] This is true in the most famous Old Testament passage about the cross, Isaiah 53. Note the particular and definite language in verses 4-6 where the people of God marvel at the Servant's work for them:[46]

> Surely he took up *our* pain
>   and bore our suffering,
> yet we considered him punished by God,
>   stricken by him, and afflicted.
> But he was pierced for *our* transgressions,
>   he was crushed for *our* iniquities;
> the punishment *that brought us peace* was on him,
>   and by his wounds *we are healed.*
> We all, like sheep, have gone astray,
>   each of us has turned to our own way;
> and the Lord has laid on him
>   the iniquity of us all. (NIV)

There are similarly definite statements in the New Testament, such as Romans 5:8-10 (we were reconciled to God by his Son's death); Galatians 1:4 (he gave himself up to deliver us, not to make deliverance a possibility), 3:13 (he redeemed us from the curse by hanging on the tree); Ephesians 1:7 (we *have* ἔχομεν, *echomen* redemption through his blood – the present tense possession of it stands out grammatically in the context); Luke 19:10 (he seeks *and*

---

[45] Though in a way that was not true for Isaac on Abraham's altar, there is obviously a gap between the accomplishment of atonement for us at the cross, and its later liberating application to us by faith.

[46] Brevard Childs, *Isaiah* (Louisville: Westminster John Knox Press, 2001), p 419 calls the whole of this poem 'the confession of the redeemed community,' although in the Hebrew of Isaiah 53:8, Isaiah refers to the Servant's work as being 'for the transgressions of *my* people (עַמִּי).' The 'all we' and 'us all' are therefore, obviously, Israel or (canonically) God's chosen people, not all people universally.

saves the lost); 1 Peter 2:24 (he definitely bore our sins, and by his wounds we were healed, not potentially healed); Hebrews 9:12 (Christ has secured eternal redemption, so it is not in doubt or contingent on something else other than his work).

As Berkhof says, in scripture 'there is an inseparable connection between the purchase and the actual bestowal of salvation'.[47] The exegetical alternative is to add caveats to all of these verses (and the many others which speak of a definite accomplishment). But would it not be clumsy to have to keep adding qualifications such as 'we potentially have redemption' or 'he gave himself up to go some way towards saving us'? Given the prevalence of this language, it seems much more sensible to conclude that definite atonement rather than indefinite atonement is the best way to avoid an unbiblical universalism.

2.2.3. *Unconditional redemption*

Third, alongside all this particular and definite language, the Bible also shows that Christ's death actually purchased and bestows on his people *the conditions for salvation.* He did not simply achieve something which they must then appropriate by the exercise of free will. He himself secured the fulfilment of the conditions which must be met. Ephesians 1:3 says we have every spiritual blessing in him. In Ephesians 2:8, 'salvation through faith' is a gift of God, both salvation and the faith required to receive it). The 'this' (τοῦτο, *touto*) in '*this* is a gift of God' is neuter, whereas 'you *have been saved* (σεσωσμένοι, *sesosmenoi*) is masculine, and 'by grace' (χάριτί, *chariti*) and 'through faith' (διὰ πίστεως, *dia pisteos*) are feminine. So the gift of God is perhaps best understood as not just salvation or faith on their own, but all that is bound up in 'salvation through faith.'[48]

---

[47] Berkhof, *Systematic Theology*, p 395. Exodus 15:16 and other passages speak of redemption as 'purchase,' so this commercial language is not imposed on the Bible from outside.

[48] Similarly, there is a *neuter* plural demonstrative in 2 Peter 1:8 (ταῦτα, *these things*) referring to the whole string of *feminine* nouns in the previous verses while in 1 Corinthians 6:11 ταῦτά refers back to a set of *masculine* nouns (as in Ephesians 5:6). See also, e.g. Genesis 38:25 (LXX) and Philippians 4:8 for masculine and feminine nouns being referred to collectively using a neuter plural.

Faith is, of course, exercised by the human recipient. Yet in scripture it is also spoken of as a gift from God. For example, in 2 Peter 1:1, our faith is *obtained* 'by the righteousness of our God and Saviour Jesus Christ.' The righteousness of our Saviour is presumably related to his obedience and saving death for us. This is what obtains our faith, quite apart from our own efforts.[49] In verse 3, therefore, surely faith is included as one of those things pertaining to life and godliness which God's divine power has given us. Indeed, we also read in Philippians 1:29 that our faith is 'granted' (ἐχαρίσθη, *echaristhe*, literally 'graced') to us 'for the sake of Christ,' and in Acts 14:27 and 18:27 people believe through grace, because God opens the door.

The fact that faith is a gift is also implied from the fact that before God makes us alive we are spiritually dead (Ephesians 2:1, 5), not just sick or weak. Dead people cannot respond or take any spiritual action. So we need God to give us faith, to give us the ability to open our hands to receive his gift.[50] Such teaching can also be seen in Acts 5:31, 11:18 and 2 Timothy 2:25 (repentance is something granted by God not worked up from within). Acts 13:48 ('as many as were appointed to eternal life believed') links our faith to our election by God.[51] In Titus 3:4-6 the application of redemption (regeneration) is also said to flow out of the work of Christ as Saviour.

So, as one scholar puts it, 'the principle of including faith in the benefits procured by Christ's death logically requires the doctrine

---

[49] Friberg's *Analytical Greek Lexicon* says that the word for *obtained* (λαχοῦσιν) refers to something which 'comes to someone always apart from his own efforts.' Louw and Nida, *Greek-English Lexicon of the New Testament Based on Semantic Domains* adds that it also carries 'the implication that the process is related somehow to divine will or favor.'

[50] See P.T. O'Brien, *The Letter to the Ephesians* (Leicester: Apollos, 1999), p 175. H.W. Hoehner, *Ephesians: An Exegetical Commentary* (Grand Rapids: Baker, 2002), pp 340-344 avoids this conclusion of his own exegesis because he has a prior commitment to the idea that 'the salvation that was purchased by Christ's death is universal in its provision' (p 341).

[51] Peterson, *Acts*, p 399 affirms this as an unqualified statement of absolute predestination, even affirming that those who do not believe are appointed to death (i.e. double predestination). God uses the proclamation of the gospel to call out the elect and save them, enabling them to believe.

of limited atonement.'[52] If faith is not a gift but something required to make a supposedly universal atonement 'active' or efficacious, then it may also be asked whether this changes the nature of faith itself. As Dutch theologians van Genderen and Velema put it, if faith 'is no longer receptive with respect to salvation in Christ, but is given a creative role in making salvation effective... Faith then becomes work that needs to be added to the work completed by Christ, who has done everything for us already.'[53]

2.2.4. *It is typical God*

Finally, there are also typological arguments for limited atonement. In Matthew 26 (amongst other places), Jesus' death is equated to that of the Passover lamb (verses 17-19 and 26-28). Yet the Passover lamb in Exodus 12 was not sacrificed for the unbelieving Egyptians, but only for the people God had chosen. Egyptians could join that people and partake of the lamb, but it was not sacrificed for Egyptians *qua* Egyptians. As Alec Motyer writes, explaining the details of the Exodus narrative itself, 'the sole purpose and use of the lamb was to provide Passover cover and Passover nourishment for the people whose number and needs it matched, and once that had been achieved, it was not available for anything or anyone else. It was chosen precisely for the people and having met their needs, had no other purpose or function so nothing of it was to remain once the meal was over.'[54] Hence Christ is said to be *our* Passover lamb (1 Corinthians 5:7).

A similar argument could be constructed for the sacrificial system generally: the burnt and peace offerings for instance are made for a particular individual who presses a hand on the animal (Leviticus 1:4, 3:2).[55] The intention, therefore, is to make atonement for that individual and them alone. If Christ fulfils these Levitical offerings, then we can assume the intentionality of his offering is also similarly focused and not 'unlimited.'

---

[52]   R. Lum, *Brief Treatise on Predestination and Its Dependent Principles by Moyse Amyraut: A Translation and Introduction* (Unpublished DTh dissertation, Dallas Theological Seminary, 1985), p iv.

[53]   Van Genderen and Velema, *Concise Reformed Dogmatics*, p 528.

[54]   *The Message of Exodus: The Days of Our Pilgrimage* (Leicester: IVP, 2005), p 136.

[55]   See G.J. Wenham, *The Book of Leviticus* (Grand Rapids: Eerdmans, 1979), pp 61-62 on this part of the ritual.

Similarly utilising Old Testament types, Jesus is presented in the New Testament as our Great High Priest, as a Davidic King, and as the Son of Man. The High Priest atoned and interceded for God's people not for everyone in the world. Leviticus 16:17 says he 'made atonement for (בְּעַד *ba'ad*, on behalf of) himself and for his house and for all the assembly of Israel.' Ezra 6:20 says of the priests and Levites generally that 'they slaughtered the Passover lamb for (לְ *l*, for, with regard to) all the returned exiles, for their fellow priests, and for themselves.' They did not, it seems, offer a sacrifice for or on behalf of anyone except God's people. In the same way, King David won his victories for the benefit of God's people rather than for, say, the Philistines (e.g. 2 Samuel 5:17-25). In Psalm 2 those who do not 'kiss the Son', that is, the Davidic king, are broken, face his wrath, and perish. Salvation is for everyone under the Son, not everyone under the sun, we might say![56] Finally, the other great Old Testament figure Jesus identifies himself with in the Gospels, the Son of Man, received a kingdom for the saints, not for the beasts (Daniel 7). These typological arguments may not be decisive, but they are certainly suggestive, and seem to indicate that the work of the Messiah was always destined to be focused on his people. It was particularly for us and for our salvation that he came down from heaven.

These four arguments then, from the focus of Christ's work, the definiteness of it, the unconditional nature of it, and the Old Testament patterns of it, persuade many that the atonement is personal, ecclesial, effective, and particular.

2.3. *Logical arguments against limited atonement*

We began this chapter looking at the logical arguments used to defend limited atonement and then moved to examine the biblical defence given for such arguments. Similarly, as we have already seen, those who hold to universal atonement often use logical arguments in their rebuttal of the case for definite atonement. Grudem puts their case succinctly:

Non-Reformed people argue that the gospel offer in Scripture

---

[56]   P.G. Feenstra, *Unspeakable Comfort: A Commentary on the Canons of Dort* (Winnipeg: Premier Publishing, 1997), p 66

is repeatedly made to all people, and for this offer to be genuine, the payment for sins must have already been made and must be actually available for all people. They also say that if the people whose sins Christ paid for are limited, then the free offer of the gospel also is limited, and the offer of the gospel cannot be made to all mankind without exception.[57]

This sort of reasoning often lies behind objections to limited atonement. They are, however, based on false deductions. The first usually insists that the offer must be 'genuine' (although this is not always well defined) without explicitly stating why. It has therefore imported a test of orthodoxy from somewhere and must justify it. It also assumes that for 'genuineness', payment must already have been made, which does not follow. Not that this is a complete illustration, but I regularly offer, quite genuinely, to take my wife to the cinema but do not always pay in advance! Besides, Roger Nicole argues that the offer is perfectly sincere: *if* anyone repents and believes they *will* be saved. Definite atonement actually undergirds such a sincere offer by providing a real rather than hypothetical salvation.[58]

Reformed theologians absolutely agree with the premise that the offer of the gospel is to be made to all.[59] They provide a number of explanations of how this is compatible with limited atonement. They might argue, for instance, that we do not know who is elect (it is a mystery reserved for God alone) so we must tell everyone, or that universal proclamation exposes the inexcusableness of those who hear and reject the gospel.[60] Or they simply say something such as,

---

[57] Grudem, *Systematic Theology*, p 594. Grudem is not Arminian of course, but his summary here is corroborated by statements in Arminian texts such as Miethe, 'The Universal Power of the Atonement', pp 83-84 and *The Arminian Confession of 1621* (Eugene: Pickwick Publications, 2005). Cf. also the same connections made by Calamy, a hypothetical universalist, in the Westminster Assembly's debate on limited atonement in C.B. Van Dixhoorn, 'Reforming the Reformation: Theological Debate at the Westminster Assembly 1642-1652' (Ph.D. diss., University of Cambridge, 2004), 6: p 205 (fo. 105r).

[58] R. Nicole, 'Covenant, Universal Call and Definite Atonement' in *Journal of the Evangelical Theological Society* 38/3 (Sept 1995), pp 403-412. Cf. Turretin, *Institutes* 2.14.XIV.liii.

[59] See for example Murray, 'The Atonement and the Free Offer', pp 60, 81.

[60] The arguments of Price and Lightfoot at the Westminster Assembly. Van Dixhoorn, 'Reforming the Reformation', 6: p 207 (fo. 106r).

'God commands all people to repent in Acts 17:30, so we should proclaim this too – even if we can't quite rationalise how that coheres with what we think is the equally biblical doctrine of limited atonement.' We should promptly and wholeheartedly obey the Lord, even if we do not entirely understand all the reasons for his commands.[61] We do know that God, in his perfect foreknowledge and fore-ordination, has made provision for everyone who believes, so that they will be saved.

Calvinist theologians have shown that on the issue of divine sovereignty and human choice, 'holding that the universe is determined... doesn't make deliberation impotent'.[62] It is often a matter of whether we consider salvation from a divine or a human perspective, and the Bible does both. In the same way, it is possible to say (from the divine angle) that Christ died for his chosen people only, while still (from the human angle) holding out the promise of salvation to all who would believe. Yet all would admit that it is difficult for our human minds to take in both perspectives at once. A forced rational consistency and exhaustive explanation is not, therefore, the *sine qua non* of the Reformed doctrine. Indeed, Arminians and hypothetical universalists are often much more strained and mechanical in their subtle distinctions on these points.[63] As Jonathan Moore and others have noted historically, it was 'the universal redemptionists who availed themselves most of scholastic distinctions, whereas it was the strict and particular redemptionists who upheld an Augustinian simplicity in their soteriology.'[64]

---

[61] Cf. Cunningham, *Historical Theology*, 2: p 345.

[62] See B. Cooper, 'Divine vs. Human Choices: Relieving the Tension with some Choice Theory' at http://www.theologian.org.uk/doctrine/DivinevsHuman Choices.html.

[63] H.C. Hoeksema, *The Voice of Our Fathers: An Exposition of the Canons of Dordrecht* (Grand Rapids: Reformed Free Publishing Association, 1980), p 339 speaks of the 'mechanical way in which the Arminians presented the work of Christ and made separation in that work.'

[64] Moore, *English Hypothetical Universalism*, p 222 n19. See also D. Sinnema, 'Reformed Scholasticism and the Synod of Dort', in B.J. van der Walt (ed.), *John Calvin's Institutes: His Opus Magnum* (Potchefstroom: Institute for Reformational Studies, 1986), p 487 and R.A. Muller, *God, Creation, and Providence in the Thought of Jacob Arminius* (Grand Rapids: Baker, 1991), p 189.

We could look at it this way: From an earthly perspective, it is fine for us to say that the sun rises and sets. We know, from a divine perspective, that it is the earth which actually does the moving and rotates around the sun. In the same way, it is fine from our human perspective for us to say, '*whoever* believes will be saved.' Yet we also know from the scriptures that God intended from the start only to save the elect. We have both views, and as long as we do not confuse them by saying God is unsure who will believe or that he intended to save everybody or that we can only evangelise certain people, then all will be well.

One would not stand on the moon and say, 'Look how the sun goes around the earth.' It would be strange for us to stare at the sky from earth and exclaim, 'Look how we are rotating around the sun.' In the same way, God's promises to us here should not be confused with his heavenly intentions. Just because God sovereignly gives a command or a promise does not mean that everyone has the ability to obey and fulfil it. Genre considerations are important here: when the genre of scripture is preaching, for example, the human-level promises are majored on; when the genre is sober theological reflection, the divine-level eternal plan comes into view. There is no contradiction here, but the two perspectives must be kept in their proper relations.[65]

This may seem paradoxical but it must also be remembered that 'God's sovereignty is no revealed rule for our action.'[66] We do not know who is elect and who is not. As Anglican Article 17 puts it, 'that Will of God is to be followed, which we have expressly declared unto us in the word of God.' So if the word says preach to all, we preach to all, even if we cannot reconcile in our heads how promiscuous preaching tallies with equally clear teaching on God's sovereignty. Ours is not to reason why, in some ways, but simply to live and die for the spread of the gospel and the glory of God.

---

[65] Calvin deals helpfully with this issue in *Institutes* 3.22.10. Cf. *Institutes* 3.24.8, 17. See also R.A. Muller, 'A Tale of Two Wills? Calvin and Amyraut on Ezekiel 18:23,' in *Calvin Theological Journal* 44.2 (2009), p 218. See also Lombard's contrast between the love of the 'fatherland' and that 'of the way' in *Sentences* 3.31.3.

[66] R.L. Dabney, *Systematic Theology* (Edinburgh: Banner of Truth, 1985), p 527.

The second objection (that if the number whose sins Christ paid for is limited, then the free offer of the gospel also must be limited) is basically a hyper-calvinist error. It is denied by mainstream proponents of effective atonement who claim that the conclusion does not necessarily follow from the premise. It is not, therefore, an essential component of the doctrine of limited atonement at all, being contradicted by the explicit teaching and practice of Calvinist evangelists such as Spurgeon and Whitefield.[67] It would be ironic to find Arminians or Amyraldians agreeing with the basic premise of a hyper-calvinist non-sequitur! Many seem unaware that for all their protestations against logic, this oft-used argument against limited atonement is itself an attempt at using logic in order to determine doctrine.[68] It should be more freely confessed that those who dislike limited atonement are just as likely, if not more so, to indulge in *logical* arguments like this. William S. Sailer, for example, claims in his Wesleyan approach to the atonement to 'confine discussion in so far as possible to relevant biblical data', but his next two pages are full of logic, including the invocation of *reductio ad absurdum* and a discussion of the Aristotelian principle of subalternation![69]

Both of these logical arguments seem to suggest that a limitation in the design of salvation must imply a limitation in the offer of the gospel. Yet even Arminians would not say that limited *election* must equal limited gospel offer. I do not think these logical assertions can be made with any kind of scriptural warrant. John Murray was even so bold as to turn these objections on their head, asserting that only limited atonement supplies the basis required for a universal offer of the gospel because it alone offers not just the general love of God or the opportunity of salvation, but salvation itself – a definite, accomplished, effective salvation.[70]

---

[67] Spurgeon's view can be seen in 'Particular Redemption' (Sermon 181) in *New Park Street Pulpit* (Edinburgh: Banner of Truth, 1964), Volume 4. Whitefield's view can be seen in *A Letter to Some Church-Members of the Presbyterian Persuasion* (1740), and e.g. Sermon 46 in L. Gatiss (ed.), *The Sermons of George Whitefield* (Watford: Church Society, 2010), Volume 2.

[68] On this see D. Macleod, 'Amyraldus Redivivus: A Review Article' in *Evangelical Quarterly* 81.3 (July 2009), p 222.

[69] W.S. Sailer, 'The Nature and Extent of the Atonement - a Wesleyan View' in *Bulletin of the Evangelical Theological Society* 10.4 (1967), pp 190-191.

[70] Murray, 'The Atonement and the Free Offer', p 83.

2.4. *Exegetical arguments against limited atonement*

Theological controversy often drives us to use arguments which seem polemically effective, rather than to search for judgments which are true. For the latter we must turn to the scriptures, of course, and not logic alone. Yet even here there are dangers. As a wise man once wrote:

> We may observe how impossible it is for men, even of the greatest learning and piety, to interpret Scripture with success, when they come to it prepossessed with systems, which they are listed, as it were, to defend. For instead of searching candidly the true meaning of the text, they come provided with senses which they are obliged to ingraft upon it; until by a practice and habit of wresting the Scripture on all occasions, they acquire a dexterity of extracting what doctrines they please out of it.[71]

This sounds very much like the accusation sometimes made against Calvinist exegesis of the 'problem texts' for limited atonement.[72] I first came across it in a passage by a staunch Calvinist against an acclaimed Arminian![73] The point remains, however, that whichever side we happen to prefer in such a debate, we must always beware of trying to impose a forced consistency upon the text, and becoming so attached to our systems that we fail to listen carefully to the word of God. One side may accuse the other of twisting scripture to make it 'fit', while itself being guilty of a simplistic, proof-texting use of the Bible which looks no deeper than the surface meaning of texts which appear to be 'on their side'. Nevertheless, as I said above, these 'problem' texts are often precisely those parts of the word which prompt Christians to start thinking about this issue in the first place. Rather than being 'enemies' to be overcome or sidelined, they are

---

[71] *The Posthumous Works of the Late Learned Conyers Middleton* (London, 1753), p 12 just after a criticism of Hugo Grotius, the famous Dutch Arminian commentator.

[72] I.H. Marshall, for instance, claims to be engaged in 'unprejudiced exegesis' and to be taking the Bible at 'face value' in his attack on limited atonement in 'Universal Grace and Atonement in the Pastoral Epistles,' in Pinnock, *The Grace of God*, p 52.

[73] A.M. Toplady in *The Complete Works of Augustus Toplady* (Harrisburg, Virginia: Sprinkle Publications, 1987), p 643.

catalysts and stimulants to deeper understanding, to be meditated on in both their immediate and canonical contexts.

2.4.1. *He died for all the world*

That being said, the unlimited atonement case is usually built on two main lines of exegetical argument. First, it points to those texts which affirm that Christ died for 'all' or for 'the world'. The classic examples are John 1:29 where the lamb of God is said to take away 'the sin of the world,' and 1 Timothy 2:6 where he is said to be 'a ransom for all'. These are taken to mean that 'quite obviously' the atonement was universal in intent and extent.[74] Such assertions are often accompanied by a passionate desire to evangelise and to stick close to scripture, which all sides in this debate should share. However, we must examine whether these verses do actually teach what opponents of limited atonement claim they do.[75]

Reformed commentators respond in a variety of ways to Arminian exegesis, and not always convincingly. But John Owen was right when he wrote that 'all our divines who maintaine that the elect only were redeemed effectually by Christ do yet grant that Christ dyed for all, in the Scripture sense of the word.'[76] The most persuasive counterarguments point out that both 'world' (κόσμος, *kosmos*) and 'all' (πᾶς, *pas*) should not immediately be assumed to mean 'everyone without exception', since they are used in scripture in a variety of ways, as can be seen in standard Greek lexicons.[77] As a recent monograph on the subject points out, the scholarly consensus is that πᾶς ('all'), 'is used to quantify substantives either collectively ("all as a

---

[74] Miethe, 'The Universal Power', p 80 says of 1 Timothy 4:10 ('Saviour of all men') that, 'quite obviously, this verse is saying that … Christ died for *all men.*'

[75] Those who would also argue against penal substitution too (which Arminians do not all do of course) use these texts as well, such as Belousek, *Atonement, Justice, and Peace*, p 291 who says, 'Jesus is not the universal substitute, taking the place of each human being one by one (exclusion), but rather our corporate representative, taking the place of all humanity at once (inclusion) - "once for all" (Romans 6:10).'

[76] P. Toon (ed.), *The Correspondence of John Owen* (Cambridge: James Clarke, 1970), p 165.

[77] E.g. πᾶς, πᾶσα, πᾶν §1.a.β in W.F. Arndt & F.W. Gingrich, *A Greek-English Lexicon of the New Testament and Other Early Christian Literature* (Cambridge: Cambridge University Press, 1957), p 636.

group") or distributively ("each and every single one in a group").' Sometimes it can be applied absolutely ('all without exception') and sometimes requires a limitation (meaning 'most' or 'many' or 'all kinds of'). Disagreements arise, however, in determining which way the word is used in any given text and when limitation is warranted.[78]

To show that we must be careful with this, consider various Old and New Testament examples. In Genesis 6:13, 17, God determines to destroy 'all flesh', using כֹּל (*kol*) in Hebrew, or πᾶς (*pas*) in the LXX. The context (the whole story!) shows, however, that this does not include Noah, his extended family, and the large number of animals he is told to save.[79] Luke 2:1 ('all the world should be registered') does not envisage the entire population of the planet taking part in a Roman census. Matthew 3:5-6 ('all Judea') does not mean to suggest that every single man, woman, and child in Judea without exception went out and was baptised by John, especially since Luke 7:30 explicitly says that the Pharisees and lawyers were *not* baptised by him. Acts 2:17 ('I will pour out my Spirit on all flesh') does not mean that everyone in the world was given the Holy Spirit at the first Pentecost. People reading English Bibles only may think the common phrase 'once for all' when applied to the death of Christ must settle the matter (e.g. Hebrews 7:27 and 10:10 in the ESV or 1 Peter 3:18 in the NIV). It is, however, a translation of ἅπαξ (*hapax*) or ἐφάπαξ (*ephapax*) meaning 'once' or 'once-and-for-all-time' and does not actually imply anything about who the death of Christ was intended for.

The meaning of the original Hebrew or Greek words in any particular passage must be determined by the context and not necessarily interpreted in such a way that they neatly fit into a preconceived framework devised or assumed by English speakers. Even Arminian commentators admit this when it comes to other texts

---

[78] J. William Johnston, *The Use of Πᾶς in the New Testament* (Oxford: Peter Lang, 2004), p 31. Johnston traces discussion of πᾶς back to Aristotle's *Metaphysics* 1024a, 1-10, and surveys some key New Testament examples looking for criteria for determining the sense of the word, concluding that 'There are syntactical and semantic guides that provide more help to interpretation than context alone' (p 29).

[79] See 2 Kings 8:9, 1 Chronicles 22:15, Nehemiah 13:16, Ezekiel 39:20 and Zephaniah 2:14 for similar Old Testament examples where the meaning cannot be 'all without exception.'

such as Matthew 5:3 (all kinds of evil), Acts 10:12 (all kinds of animals), Romans 7:8 (all kinds of covetousness) or 1 Timothy 6:10 (money is a root of all kinds of evil) where the word is from the same root (πᾶς, *pas*).[80] In John 12:19 no-one seriously thinks the entire population of earth was following Jesus.[81] So it cannot be simply assumed to mean 'all without exception' in places such as 1 Timothy 2:6. Context must always be taken into account, to establish the implied sphere of reference. We do this in ordinary English, of course: I arrive at a lecture and ask, 'Is everyone here?' I do not mean 'Is every single person in the universe now present?' Everyone (*sic*) knows this!

There is testimony to a very long tradition of exegesis, from Augustine and Aquinas to Luther and Calvin, which understands 'all' in 1 Timothy 2:4-6, for example, as 'all kinds of' rather than 'all without exception'.[82] Even if all this is discounted, however, in 1 Timothy 2:4 we must (as Calvinists and Arminians can agree), 'certainly distinguish between what God would like to see happen and what he actually does will to happen.'[83] The standard terminology for this distinction is God's 'revealed will' and 'secret will' or 'will of command' and 'will of decree' or 'moral will' and 'sovereign will.'[84] Just because God wishes all to be saved, in some sense, does not mean he has, in another sense, actually willed to save them all by

---

[80]   On 1 Timothy 6:10, I.H. Marshall, *The Pastoral Epistles* (London: T&T Clark, 1999), p 651 says that it is hyperbole. J.N.D. Kelly, *The Pastoral Epistles* (London: A&C Black, 1963), p 138 claims that it is better translated 'all kinds of evil'. Neither opts for a hyperbolic or 'all kinds of' interpretation of the same word (πᾶς) in 1 Timothy 2:4 or 2:6. Calvinist commentator George Knight, *The Pastoral Epistles*, pp 257-258 sees the same sense in 2:4, 2:6, 4:10, and 6:10 but his first consideration in the latter is the immediate context of 6:9.

[81]   See the helpful note in L. Morris, *The Gospel According to John: Revised* (Grand Rapids: Eerdmans, 1995), pp 111-113.

[82]   Augustine, *Enchiridion* 27, 103; Aquinas, *Summa Theologiae* 1, Q.19, art.6 gives it as a possibility; Luther, *Lectures on Romans*, scholia in Romans 8, II; Calvin, *Calvin's Commentaries Volume XXI* (Grand Rapids: Baker, 1993), pp 54-55, 57 (on 1 Timothy 2:4-6). See also Gottschalk, *On Predestination*, 9 and *Reply to Rabanus Maurus*, pp 6-7.

[83]   The words of an Arminian —Marshall, 'Universal Grace and Atonement in the Pastoral Epistles', 56 – heartily agreed with by Calvinist John Piper in 'Are There Two Wills in God?' in Schreiner and Ware, *Sovereign Grace*, p 110.

[84]   Cf. Reymond, *A New Systematic Theology*, pp 692-693 who rejects this 'two wills' argument.

designing and providing a universal atonement. He certainly has not *elected* all – so scripture itself forces us to make careful distinctions here and to find some way of reconciling these two things. Unless, of course, we wish to take the easy route and abandon the Protestant hermeneutic of 'scripture must interpret scripture.'[85]

Hebrews 2:9 is sometimes quoted against limited atonement: 'he tasted death for everyone/all.'[86] In the immediate context of the passage itself, however, it is clear that this work was focused on those who will be brought to glory, the sanctified, Jesus' 'brothers,' those who put their trust in him, his children, 'the people' (Hebrews 2:10-17).[87] More widely, Hebrews 9:15 and 9:28 show that Hebrews operates with the idea of a definite atonement which actually redeems only a specific group of people, the 'many.' He died specifically to sanctify them (Hebrews 13:12). So it seems most natural to conclude that Jesus really died and had a thorough taste of death for all those whom God will finally bring to glory thereby. The word 'all' in Hebrews 2:9, when not wrenched out of its context and made to bear more weight than it can carry, clearly does not mean every individual without exception. Ben Witherington claims there is 'little doubt' that the writer of Hebrews wanted to stress that Jesus did not die just for the elect.[88] Yet Hebrews seems clear that through his suffering, Christ became 'the source of salvation' not to all without exception but 'to all who obey him' (Hebrews 5:9). Through his priestly offering he has 'perfected for all time' not every single individual but 'those who are

---

[85] Interestingly, official Roman Catholic doctrine interprets 1 Timothy 2 in a universal atonement manner. See *Dogmatic Constitution of the Church: Lumen Gentium* (1964), chapter 2, number 16.

[86] E.g. H. Hammond, *A Paraphrase and Annotations on All the Books of the New Testament* (London, 1659), p 728 sees it as teaching that the cross is for 'the benefit of all mankind and every man in the world.'

[87] The important connection between verse 9 and verse 10 is pointed out by advocates of particular redemption from at least the ninth century, e.g. Remigius Lugdunensis, *De Tribus Epistolis Liber* in *Patrologia Latina* 121:1015a-b. P.T. O' Brien, *The Letter to the Hebrews* (Nottingham: Apollos, 2010), pp 100-102 also makes the connection, not only to show that Christ tasted death for *people* (rather than all creation) but also that the 'all' in verse 9 is 'now made more precise' in verse 10 with the phrase 'many sons and daughters.'

[88] B. Witherington, *Letters and Homilies for Jewish Christians: A Socio-Rhetorical Commentary on Hebrews, James and Jude* (Nottingham: Apollos, 2007), p 144.

being sanctified' (Hebrews 10:14). Jesus 'tastes death' for those who keep his word, so that they need never taste it themselves (John 8:52).

Commenting on Hebrews 2:9, the early biblical scholar Origen (185-254) considered Christ to have died for humanity, the fallen angels, and perhaps even the stars (because of Job 25:5)![89] In this vein, some also point to Colossians 1:20, 'through Christ, God was pleased to reconcile all things to himself, whether on earth or in the heavens, having made peace through the blood of his cross.' Does this not indicate a reconciliation of 'all things' (τὰ πάντα, *ta panta*, neuter) by Christ's blood, and hence that he died for all things?

The word for 'lost' in 'Jesus came to seek and save the lost' (Luke 19:10) is also neuter, so the grammatical observation that 'all things' in Colossians 1:20 is neuter does not necessarily mean that 'people' are not in view. The word πνεῦμα (*pneuma*, Spirit) is also neuter, but this does not mean the Holy Spirit is not a person! Hebrews 2:16 also indicates that Christ did not come to take hold of or assist angels, but people. It seems better, in any case, to read Colossians 1:20 as indicating that the cross-centred peacemaking between God and humans (specifically the church, verses 18, 21) begins by reconciling God and humans, but has a wider cosmic impact through that. It is, as Peter O'Brien says, 'the world of men which is in view.'[90] As we, the cause of the world's disruption, are put right with our creator by the blood of atonement, the creation enjoys this restoration of harmony and longs for all the elect to come in (cf. Romans 8:19-21). But Christ does not suffer for the fallen angels or for fallen creation. The verse teaches, in other words, 'not "cosmic salvation" or even "cosmic redemption," but "cosmic restoration" or "renewal."'[91]

---

[89] See Schaff, *Ante-Nicene Fathers* (Peabody: Hendrickson, 1994), 9: pp 318-319.

[90] P.T. O'Brien, *Colossians, Philemon* (Waco: Word Books, 1982), p 53. He narrows this down further on p 57 saying, 'the central purpose of Christ's work of making peace has to do with those who have heard the Word of reconciliation and gladly accepted it.'

[91] D.J. Moo, *The Letters to the Colossians and to Philemon* (Nottingham: Apollos, 2008), 136. Cf. J.D.G. Dunn, *The Epistles to the Colossians and to Philemon* (Carlisle: Paternoster, 1996), p 104 on Colossians 1:6, 10, 27, 28 and how this cosmic goal is achieved through the gospel.

Augustine's take on Colossians 1:20 was that 'The things which are in heaven are "renewed" (*instaurantur*) when what was lost in the fall of the angels is restored from among people; and the things which are on earth are "renewed" when those who are predestined to eternal life are redeemed from their old corruption.'[92] Later, Thomas Aquinas for one had no taste for speculations of astro-redemption, and saw the Nicene Creed as denying such a view when it says 'For *us*, and for *our* salvation, he came down from heaven.'[93] Even seventeenth century Arminian commentators did not necessarily see Colossians 1:20 as supporting a universal atonement, whereas confessional Calvinists considered it as absolutely in line with their understanding.[94]

When it comes to the word 'world', the most important texts to consider are John 1:29, John 3:16, and 1 John 2:2. The latter two were in fact cited in the *Remonstrance* of 1610 which contained the original five points of Arminianism, in support of universal atonement. It is unnecessary to claim that κόσμος (*kosmos*, world) here means 'a world within the world,' such as 'the elect' or 'the church.'[95] This does, however, have a very long pedigree.[96] Yet it is also unwarranted to simply assume it means 'everyone on the planet' without regard for the context. John specifically distinguishes the

---

[92] *Enchiridion*, chapter 62. On redeemed humanity taking the place of the fallen angels, see Augustine, *The City of God*, 22.1 and *Enchiridion*, 29 as well as Peter Lombard's *Sentences* 2.1.5 and 2.9.6.

[93] Aquinas, *Compendium of Theology* (Oxford: Oxford University Press, 2009), 177. Cf. Jerome's Letter 124 to Avitus in *Patrologia Latina* 22:1070. When Athanasius alludes to this text in *On Luke X.22*, section 3, he says the Saviour 'became man for the sake of saving man.'

[94] See the Arminian, Hammond, *Paraphrase and Annotations*, pp 651-652 who takes 'all things in heaven and earth' as referring to Jews and Gentiles. The Calvinist, *Westminster Confession of Faith* 8.5 cites this verse as a proof for the redemption by Christ of those 'given to him by the Father.'

[95] As e.g. George Gillespie and Samuel Rutherford (respectively) did in the Westminster Assembly's debate on limited atonement. See Van Dixhoorn, 'Reforming the Reformation,' 6: p 207 (fo. 106r) and 6: p 209 (fo. 107r). N.F. Douty, *The Death of Christ: Did Christ Die Only for the Elect?* (Irving: William & Watrous, 1978), pp 41-45 spends a great deal of time and effort showing this is lexicographically unwarranted (which is not entirely pertinent), while Carson, *The Difficult Doctrine*, pp 18-19 is not the only Reformed exegete to distance himself from such a suggestion.

[96] See T. Wells, *A Price for a People* (Edinburgh: Banner of Truth, 1992), pp 125-126.

disciples from the world (e.g. John 14:17, 15:18, 17:9), thus showing that even within the Gospel itself the term 'world' cannot mean everyone without exception.[97] Good arguments can be made for regarding John 1:29 as teaching that Christ, rather than being the sacrificial (Passover?) lamb or Suffering Servant for *Israel*, will in fact bear away sin for people all over the world, i.e. world means something like 'not just for Jews.'[98] Alternatively it could be said to refer to people generally, since only those who believe in universal salvation would argue that the sins of all people without exception are truly and actually taken away in a definite sense.[99] It may also mean that he 'came as a sin-offering bearing not his own, but the sins of others.'[100]

As for John 3:16, when examined carefully it does not actually say anything at all about the extent or intent of the atonement directly. In a sense, it is irrelevant to the argument. What John 3:16 is talking about is God's motivation in sending Jesus into the (darkness-loving, God-hating) world to die. He did it because he did not want to give up on humanity as a whole (as we hear him anthropopathically contemplating in Genesis 6:5-7) but it is not about 'a purpose to save every person in the world individually'.[101] It also speaks about the universal offer and invitation of the gospel which is not the same as (and does not have to rely on) universal atonement.[102] It does not say that God set out to save every single person in the world or that Christ 'died for' every single person in the world. It does, however, widen out the scope of God's love which is wide enough to embrace not just

---

[97] Cf. Murray, 'The Atonement and the Free Offer', p 79. See also 1 John 5:19, Revelation 12:9, 13:3 where 'whole world' cannot literally mean everyone.

[98] See Vos, 'The Scriptural Doctrine', p 450. Cf. Morris, *The Gospel According to John*, pp 127-130 for discussion of several possible allusions here and his conclusion that it is probably a composite picture of several or all Old Testament sacrifices – all of which were for *Israel's* benefit.

[99] See Grudem, *Systematic Theology*, p 598. Carson, *The Gospel According to John*, p 151 says that 'world' must mean 'all without distinction' rather than 'all without exception'.

[100] An attractive suggestion from Hodge, *Systematic Theology*, 2: p 559.

[101] Vos, 'The Scriptural Doctrine', p 443.

[102] See Calvin on John 3:16 in *Calvin's Commentaries Volume XVII* (Grand Rapids: Baker, 1993), pp 122-126 who applies it to indiscriminate gospel proclamation, and adds (p 125), 'Christ is made known and held out to the view of all, but the elect alone are they whose eyes God opens.'

Israel but the world.[103] God so loved the rebellious world that he provided a way for rebellious sinners to be saved through Christ. *Anyone* who believes in him will not perish. He is given to the world in such a way that everyone who believes is saved.[104]

This is fully consistent with the background, alluded to in John 3:14-15, of the incident with the bronze serpent. God now offers salvation through Christ not just to Israelites, suffering snake bites on their wilderness wanderings, but to the whole sinful world. This has no bearing on the specific question of whether God ultimately intended the salvation or reprobation of those to whom the salvation was offered. Indeed, in Numbers 21, the bronze serpent was proffered as salvation even to those whom God had already decreed should die in the desert at some point in that 40 year period (Numbers 14:21-23). As Andreas Köstenberger puts it, 'In Numbers 21, it was *the Jewish people* who looked with faith upon the serpent for healing, while in John 3:16 it is *the entire world* that must look to Jesus in faith for salvation.'[105] This is surely right, and avoids unwarranted conclusions about the extent of the atonement which the text simply does not address.

Marshall avers that 'it is difficult to see how one might say, "God loves you" without at the same time being able to say, "Christ died for you"... It is therefore possible and indeed necessary to affirm both of the two statements with full theological integrity.'[106] Yet this is simply asserting what one is trying to prove. As noted before, Carson and others have shown that God's love is spoken of in various ways in scripture and certainly cannot be taken in every instance to be the

---

[103]   Morris, *The Gospel According to John*, p 203. Cf. Carson, *The Gospel According to John*, p 205.

[104]   J.R. Gerstner, 'The Atonement and the Purpose of God,' in G.N.E. Fluhrer (ed.), *Atonement* (Phillipsburg: P&R, 2010), p 63 goes much further and claims John 3:16 is 'the choicest passage' in favour of limited atonement. It does seem to rely on a definiteness in the atonement: because of the cross, the salvation of believers is not *possible* or *potential* but certain and definite.

[105]   A.J. Köstenberger, 'Lifting Up the Son of Man and God's Love for the World: John 3:16 in Its Historical, Literary, and Theological Contexts,' in Andreas Köstenberger and Robert Yarbrough (eds.), *Understanding the Times: New Testament Studies in the 21st Century* (Nottingham: IVP, 2011), p 155. He says later that God gave Jesus 'to provide atonement for all the people of the world' (p 159), but it is unclear what precisely he means by 'providing' atonement.

[106]   I.H. Marshall, 'Universal Grace and Atonement in the Pastoral Epistles', p 64.

equivalent of his particular, redemptive love towards those he intends to save. Indeed, as we have already seen, John 6:38-39, alongside John 17:9, shows that Jesus was sent for a limited group of people 'given' to him by the Father. They are explicitly *not* the world, although they do include all those who will believe in future (John 17:20). There is, therefore, no scriptural or theological warrant for equating 'God so loved the world' with 'God sent Jesus because he intended to save the whole world.'[107]

Perhaps the most difficult text of this sort from a limited atonement perspective is 1 John 2:2. This explicitly says Jesus 'is the propitiation for our sins, and not for ours only but also for the sins of the whole world.' This appears on the surface to speak directly into the debate and to be decisively against limited atonement. Yet we must be careful not to jump too quickly to the conclusion that John is using these terms in the way theologians centuries later did when debating the extent of the atonement. That clearly is not the main purpose of 1 John. On this point, Don Carson argues that,

> 1 John 2:2 states something about the potential breadth of the atonement. As I understand the historical context, the proto-gnostic opponents John was facing thought of themselves as an ontological élite who enjoyed the inside track with God because of the special insight they had received. But when Jesus Christ died, John rejoins, it was not for the sake of, say, Jews only or, now, of some group, Gnostic or otherwise, that sets itself up as intrinsically superior. Far from it. It was not for our sins only, but also for the sins of the whole world. The context, then, understands this to mean something like "potentially for all without distinction" rather than "effectively for all without exception."[108]

While he would have differed in details from Carson (whose last line there may be somewhat confused), John Owen also spent careful

---

[107] See also the further argument of Murray, 'The Atonement and the Free Offer,' p 80 relating to the parallelism with John 3:17.

[108] Carson, *Difficult Doctrine*, pp 87-88. In footnote 2 on p 102, he says he has defended this as the background to 1 John 2:2 in his forthcoming commentary on the Johannine Epistles in the NIGTC series. See also Vos, 'The Scriptural Doctrine', p 450. This is a much more nuanced exegesis than that which Dabney objects to in *Systematic Theology*, p 525.

effort reconstructing the particular context of John's readers. He works out the pastoral aim and purpose of this phrase within the letter, before examining the scriptural use of the words, especially ἱλασμός (*hilasmos*, propitiation) and ὅλου τοῦ κόσμου (*holou tou kosmou*, the whole world).[109] Calvinist exegesis since at least the seventeenth century has been careful to put this verse in its context. The *Dutch Annotations*, for example, associated with the Synod of Dort, argue that 'our' in 1 John 2:2 refers to 'the Apostles and other believers who now live,' which is quite plausible in the context of 1 John 1:3, for example. They go on to say that the cross was also for the sins 'of all men in the whole world out of all Nations, who shall yet believe in him.' In support of this reading they cite John 11:52 and Revelation 5:9, which were both thought to be by the same apostle John who wrote this epistle. The clear implication is that Christ did not die for every single person but only for some 'out of' all nations.[110] Others have thought it was merely saying that there is no other propitiation, so that anyone who is saved is saved by this,[111] and Aquinas is not alone in restricting 1 John 2:2 to the *sufficiency* of the cross.[112]

By contrast, it is simply not careful exegesis to assert boldly that 'John rules out the thought that the death of Jesus is of limited efficacy' and then to quote a hymn of John Wesley which affirms the doctrine of universal atonement, as one Arminian scholar does in an otherwise weighty commentary.[113] Stephen Smalley is equally lax for importing the idea of the universal *effectiveness* of the atonement into this text without attempting to justify it.[114] It is clear then that 1 John 2:2 cannot be claimed as a knock-down verse for unlimited atonement without more serious consideration being given to the

---

[109] Owen, *Works*, 10: pp 330-338.

[110] See T. Haak, *The Dutch Annotations... Ordered and Appointed by the Synod of Dort* (London, 1657).

[111] An Augustinian thought, echoed by Tom Wells, 'For Whom Did Christ Die?' in *Reformation and Revival* 5.1 (1996), p 62 and J. Ramsey Michaels, 'Atonement in John's Gospels and Epistles,' in Hill & James, *Glory of the Atonement*, p 117.

[112] Aquinas, *Compendium of Theology*, pp 170, 190.

[113] I.H. Marshall, *The Epistles of John* (Grand Rapids: Eerdmans, 1978), p 119.

[114] S. Smalley, *1, 2, 3 John* (Waco: Word Books, 1984), p 40.

context, and to the exegesis of scholars such as Owen and Carson.[115] It should also not be used to jar against other texts which affirm a limited view, as if scripture was presenting us here with a 'tension' (usually called a contradiction) to be accepted by faith, unless it can be clearly shown to be addressing precisely the same question and not the distinguishably separate issue of universal sufficiency.

All this being said, it would be a mistake to imagine that making the intentional focus of the cross the elect is somehow a bigoted or narrow thing to do. It is far from parochial. God's plan is to recreate and bless the entire cosmos through his people. That has always been his plan and purpose in redemption, as is clear from the Pentateuch onwards. The salvation of God's people through the blood of the cross is part of his plan to unite all things in heaven and on earth in Christ (Ephesians 1:7-10). It is one thing to affirm that the redemption of the elect which God planned from before the foundation of the world has a huge significance, even beyond the borders of the church, but quite another to say that he therefore intended to redeem everyone beyond the borders of the elect. Positing a universal significance and impact for the cross does not mean it had to have a universal saving intention or extent. Indeed, in Romans 8:19-23 it seems that the more universal, creation-wide, effects of redemption are enacted precisely through a particular redemption of the 'children of God.'

2.4.2. *Apostasy and the Fruitless Cross*

The second main pillar of the case for universal atonement is the so-called apostasy texts. Romans 14:15 and 1 Corinthians 8:11 have already been cited above as part of the argument for limited atonement. They show that when Paul appeals to the idea that Christ died *for* someone (ὑπὲρ οὗ, *huper hou*, or δι'ὅν, *di'hon*) that 'someone' is always a Christian *brother* (ἀδελφός, *adelphos*), a family member rather than someone who has not come to faith. These verses are, however, sometimes also cited on the opposing side of the

---

[115]   Cf. also the argument of Grudem, *Systematic Theology*, pp 598-599 concerning the ambiguity of the περι+ genitive construction and the additional arguments in J. Murray, *Redemption Accomplished and Applied* (Edinburgh: Banner of Truth, 1955), pp 72-75.

debate to show 'the fruitlessness of the blood of Christ,'[116] because they allegedly affirm that a person for whom Christ died could be 'destroyed' (from ἀπόλλυμι, *apollumi*) and hence could not be elect.

There is disagreement in the commentators over what 'destroyed' signifies here: on 1 Corinthians 8:11 for instance, Gordon Fee avers that 'Paul most likely is referring to eternal loss.' Craig Blomberg, on the other hand, seems equally sure that, 'it is doubtful if Paul could imagine that these inherently amoral issues could actually jeopardize a Christian's salvation'.[117] On Romans 14:15 Douglas Moo agrees with Fee about the probability of ἀπόλλυμι (*apollumi*) signifying ultimate spiritual ruin. Yet he also suggests that Paul might be exaggerating, that the person is not said to be genuinely regenerate, and that Paul does not say the destruction will actually take place (i.e. it is a warning).[118] John Stott on the other hand thinks there are several reasons in the context against seeing ἀπόλλυμι (*apollumi*) in Romans 14:15 as final eschatological ruin.[119] The unlimited atonement case, however, is that such apostasy texts show that Christ died for those who will finally fall away, i.e. the non-elect.[120] He died for them, but in vain. Reformed commentators who think that to die *for* someone means to actually save them might say that on this Arminian theory, Christ actually died for no-one![121]

The most important of these apostasy texts is arguably 2 Peter 2:1 where Peter says that false prophets 'will secretly introduce destructive heresies/factions, even denying the Master who bought them, bringing upon themselves imminent destruction'. This is cited by opponents of particular atonement as being one of the key texts on

---

[116] An arresting phrase from Owen, *Works*, 10: p 359.

[117] Fee, *The First Epistle to the Corinthians* (Grand Rapids: Eerdmans, 1987), p 387; Blomberg, *1 Corinthians* (Grand Rapids: Zondervan, 1994), p 163.

[118] *The Epistle to the Romans* (Grand Rapids: Eerdmans, 1996), pp 854-855. He is incorrect in note 28 to say advocates of limited atonement *must* conclude the person spoken of in Romans 14:15 is genuinely regenerate.

[119] *The Message of Romans: God's Good News for the World* (Leicester: IVP, 1994), pp 365-366.

[120] See, for example, Knox, 'Some Aspects,' p 263. Cf. F. Guy, 'The Universality of God's Love' in Pinnock, *The Grace of God*, p 49 n31 who sees these texts as limiting the effectiveness of the atonement, though he considers the described result (i.e. destruction) to be 'apparent hyperbole.'

[121] E.g. W. Twisse, *The Doctrine of the Synod of Dort and Arles, Reduced to the Practise* (Amsterdam, 1631), pp 16-17.

their side, since it appears to say that Christ bought (presumably with his death) some who will not make it to the new creation.[122] So, for instance, J.C. Ryle writes that:

> I believe it is possible to be more systematic than the Bible in our statements. When I read that the wicked who are lost, "deny the Lord that bought them" (2 Peter ii.1)... I dare not confine the intention of redemption to the saints alone.[123]

It might of course be possible to argue that ἀπώλειαν (*apoleian*, destruction) does not refer to the loss of eternal salvation, as with the cognate verb ἀπόλλυμι (*apollumi*) in 1 Corinthians 8:11 and Romans 14:15.[124] Hence, those who deny the Master who bought them are not really 'destroyed' eternally; this is perhaps mere hyperbole based on the word-play with '*destructive* heresies', and intended as a warning to some who are false teachers yet still truly Christians. Yet even if ἀπώλεια (*apoleia*) can have a wider semantic range,[125] it would seem to have an eternal dimension in 2 Peter itself (e.g. 2 Peter 3:7 where it is linked with the Day of Judgment). Similarly, the language of denial here alludes to Jesus' words in Matthew 10:33 ('whoever denies me...') with the terrifying eschatological result described there ('I also will deny').[126]

Equally, possible but relatively implausible are attempts to limit the meaning of 'bought' (ἀγοράσαντα, *agorasanta*) to a non-

---

[122] See A.D. Chang, 'Second Peter 2:1 and the Extent of the Atonement' in *Bibliotheca Sacra* 142 (1985), pp 52-61 against limited atonement, versus D.W. Kennard, 'Petrine Redemption: Its Meaning And Extent' in *Journal of the Evangelical Theological Society* 30/4 (December 1987), pp 399-405 in favour of it.

[123] J.C. Ryle, *Expository Thoughts on John*, 1: pp 61-62. See also Knox, 'Some Aspects,' pp 263 and 266 as well as Lightner, *The Death Christ Died*, p 15 and Miethe (quoting Millard Erickson), 'The Universal Power', p 92.

[124] That is Reymond's basic argument on those texts in *A New Systematic Theology*, pp 698-700.

[125] See Louw and Nida, *Greek-English Lexicon of the New Testament Based on Semantic Domains* under definitions 20.31 and 65.14 which give possible meanings of destroy or waste/ruin (e.g. Mark 14:4 and Luke 5:37). Cf. the discussion of H-C Hahn, 'ἀπώλεια' in C. Brown (ed.), *The New International Dictionary of New Testament Theology* (Carlisle: Paternoster, 1986), 1: pp 462-465. Clearly it does not always mean eternal destruction; context remains vital for determining the meaning.

[126] Cf. 2 Timothy 2:12.

salvific purchasing.[127] It does seem that the New Testament invariably has salvation in mind when this word is used in association with Christ.[128] Marshall helpfully notes that the word for Master (δεσπότης, *despotes*) is often used of a master of slaves (e.g. I Timothy 6:1-2; Titus 2:9; I Peter 2:18) and so the purchase in view could well be that of slaves who change ownership.[129] This would chime in very well with the approach taken by the authors of *Pierced for our Transgressions* who, after pointing out that redemption language has significant Old Testament roots in the exodus from slavery in Egypt, go on to say,

> Yet I Corinthians 10:1-10 reminds us that some who experienced this outwardly did not enjoy the blessings of final salvation... some who *outwardly* experienced the blessings of the Christian life were not truly born again. Thus being "bought" in 2 Peter 2:1 most likely refers to this outward perspective, and need not imply that those guilty of "denying the sovereign Lord" had been *inwardly* redeemed.[130]

Tom Schreiner's interpretation works along the same lines:

> I would suggest that Peter used phenomenological language... Peter said that they were bought by Jesus Christ, in the sense that they gave every indication initially of genuine faith. In every church there are members who appear to be believers and who should be accepted as believers according to the

---

[127] Classically, Owen, *Works*, 10: pp 363-364 and Turretin, *Institutes* 2.14.XIV.xliii who equates it with the limited redemption of sorts described for these people in 2 Peter 2:20-21. Cf. Reymond, *A New Systematic Theology*, pp 700-701 and G.D. Long, *Definite Atonement* (Nutley: P&R, 1976), pp 72-77.

[128] E.g. I Corinthians 6:20, 7:23; I Peter 1:18-19; Revelation 5:9, 14:3-4. See T.R. Schreiner, *1, 2 Peter, Jude* (Nashville: Broadman & Holdman, 2003), p 330. Some small doubt remains since, as Owen and Long point out, there is usually some reference to the price paid (e.g. the blood of Christ) in soteriological uses. Owen also expresses doubts as to whether their δεσπότης, master, is Christ.

[129] I.H. Marshall, 'The Development of the Concept of Redemption,' in R.J. Banks (ed.), *Reconciliation and Hope* (Exeter: Paternoster, 1974), p 159 (and see footnote I on that page).

[130] Jeffery, Ovey, and Sach, *Pierced for our Transgressions*, p 275 n78. Cf. Owen, *Works*, 10: p 362 contrasting reality with apprehension and profession; Turretin, *Institutes* 2.14.XIV.xliv contrasting internal, spiritual, and real with external and apparent as to profession; and Grudem's similar approach to different texts in *Systematic Theology*, p 599.

judgment of charity. As time elapses and difficulties arise, it becomes apparent that they are wolves in the flock (Acts 20:29-30), that though they called on Jesus as Lord their disobedience shows that he *never* knew them.[131]

On the same lines we should certainly note that the people in view in 2 Peter 2:1 are not 'unbelievers' generally. They are not the God-hating outside world which unlimited atonement advocates would like to address with the news that Christ died for them. They are professing Christians, members of the church (they are 'among you', ἐν ὑμῖν, *en humin*), and even leaders. This verse does not refer to people in general who potentially could benefit from the atonement if only they would believe, and so it cannot prove quite as much as Arminian or 'four point Calvinist' interpreters would like it to. D.G. McCartney even goes as far as to say that, 'since Peter gives no indication whatever that all people without distinction are the slaves of Christ, the reference to Christ's purchasing of "them" as his slaves supports rather than denies the definiteness of the atonement.'[132]

Certainly what it does show, like Romans 14:15 and 1 Corinthians 8:11, is that professing Christians within the church (whatever their ultimate eternal destiny or true spiritual state might be) can be spoken of in scripture as if they were beneficiaries of the salvation won for the decretally elect on the cross.[133] Indeed, professing Christians are said by Paul to be 'chosen by God' in 1 Thessalonians 1:4. He knows their election (from ἐκλογη, *ekloge,* the same word as in Romans 9:11). Assuming that Paul, even as an

---

[131] Schreiner, *1, 2 Peter, Jude,* p 331 (emphasis original). See his similar argument in his *Romans,* 735 n17 on Romans 14:15 which he says is not an argument for the truly elect being lost, since Paul 'refers to believers phenomenologically, that is, at the level of appearances, rather than at the level of true spiritual reality.' See the same general approach to this text in R.B. Kuiper, *For Whom Did Christ Die?* (Grand Rapids: Eerdmans, 1959), p 38.

[132] D.G. McCartney, 'Atonement in James, Peter and Jude,' in Hill and James, *The Glory of the Atonement,* p 179.

[133] Some may see the change of ownership in view here as that which occurred when these people were baptised: they then covenantally belonged to Jesus, but may not have been truly regenerated, thus making the sort of distinction made by Charles Simeon, for example, when he says in *Helps to Composition; or, Six Hundred Skeletons of Sermons* (Philadelphia, 1810), 3: p 92 that 'We are indeed received into covenant with God in baptism; but it is regeneration that really makes us his children.'

apostle, did not have special infallible knowledge of their individual elect/non-elect status, it is plausible to conclude that this is phenomenological language of some kind, based on appearances and ascribing to them, as a group perhaps, what may only have been true *decretally* (eternally) of a proportion of them. Of course, we know from elsewhere that being phenomenologically part of the community of faith does not guarantee eternal salvation, as Matthew 7:21-23 makes very clear. Yet even if 'the church' can in some contexts be said to be elect beneficiaries of the work of Christ, this falls far short of demonstrating that everybody on the planet can be spoken of (or to) in that same way.[134]

Moreover, as Schreiner astutely points out, 'The entire discussion on limited atonement in this verse cannot be segregated from the issue of whether believers can truly apostatize.'[135] Many commentators on Romans 14:15 would also see the big doctrinal issue in that text not as unlimited atonement (which, after all, is supposed to focus on *unbelievers* and all indiscriminately) but as the perseverance of the saints.[136] These things are of course connected (as all the petals of this particular TULIP are) but the biggest issue in 2 Peter 2 is the non-perseverance and ultimate condemnation of some who outwardly may sound like believers. They were teachers of the church, feasting with them, outwardly identified with true believers, and holding out the promise of freedom to others – and yet their immoral, licentious lifestyle was a tacit denial of Christ's ownership of them and contradicted the 'way of righteousness' they knew. If, however, we reject the language of outward appearance and say that Christ truly and absolutely atoned for their sin (rather than 'bought them' phenomenologically speaking) then the real question is what becomes of the guarantee of their preservation and final inheritance?

That is a question outside the scope of this study, but interestingly it is very much in Peter's sights later in the same chapter (2 Peter 2:20-22). Peter teaches that those who are genuinely granted

---

[134] Gottschalk, *On Predestination*, 4-6 is unusual in the force with which he speaks against saying Christ died for the 'baptised reprobate.'

[135] Schreiner, *1, 2 Peter, Jude*, p 330.

[136] Which is the doctrinal issue raised regarding Romans 14:15 by Stott, *Romans*, p 366; L. Morris, *The Epistle to the Romans* (Leicester: IVP, 1988), p 487 n58; Schreiner, *Romans*, p 735 n17.

faith (2 Peter 1:1) are effectually called by God's glory and granted everything required for life and godliness (2 Peter 1:3). The 'elect exiles' are sprinkled with Christ's blood, born again, and will be preserved by God's power for an imperishable heavenly inheritance (1 Peter 1:1-5). And yet on some readings of 2 Peter 2:1 all this is called into question because someone for whom Christ died, someone who was sprinkled with his blood and truly regenerated, will be eternally condemned and fail to enter the eternal kingdom of our Lord and Saviour Jesus Christ. The only convincing way I have found to avoid this conclusion is to deny that 2 Peter 2:1 is talking about a real inward and effective redemption for such people.[137] As Murray puts it, 'The non-elect enjoy many benefits that accrue *from* the atonement but they do not partake of the *atonement*.'[138] Truly effective atonement is reserved for the truly elect, by God's design.

In one sense, the exercise above has been somewhat unfair. As Wesleyan theologian William Sailer puts it, 'Reformed exegetes have the task of demonstrating that *every* apparently universal passage is in reality limited. The Arminian, on the other hand, need find but a single passage indicating universal atonement in order to maintain his view.'[139] However, I am convinced, with Charles Simeon, that if many extreme Calvinists or Arminians had been with the apostle Paul while he was writing they would both have suggested a few changes to his phraseology as they glanced over his shoulder![140] There are 'problem texts' for both sides. Yet if one or two problematic passages may vex or elude us still (and I have hardly accounted for every single one in this brief survey), that is a call to continued prayerful engagement with them. This is how God designed his word to work. It should not, however, cause too many sleepless nights if the central thrust of scripture's teaching on the subject has been adequately established.

I conclude, therefore, that there is a strong positive case for limited atonement, properly defined, in the Bible itself. Moreover, this position has greater explanatory power when it comes to the apparently universal texts and the apostasy passages than alternative

---

[137] Cf. McCartney, 'Atonement in James, Peter and Jude', p 179 n5.
[138] Murray, 'The Atonement and the Free Offer,' p 69 (emphasis original).
[139] Sailer, 'Nature and Extent,' pp 191-192.
[140] C. Simeon, *Horae Homileticae* (London, 1819), 1: pp 5-6.

interpretations, which often create more problems than they solve and are not as contextually sensitive. The weight of the paradigm thus established should therefore convince us that Christ did not die in vain, and his atonement bore fruit for those he came to save. Therefore, I believe that we can wholeheartedly join with the songwriter who says, 'I will trust in the cross of my Redeemer, I will sing of the blood *that never fails.*'[41]

---

[41] 'Beautiful Saviour' by Stuart Townend. Copyright © 1998 Thankyou Music.

3. HISTORICAL AND DOCTRINAL DEVELOPMENTS

In this section, we will do a quick tour of church history to see where this issue has arisen before. We will then pause for a more in-depth look at the major areas of contention in the sixteenth and seventeenth centuries, especially the view of John Calvin, the Synod of Dort and the Westminster Assembly, hypothetical universalism's 'middle way,' and the question of whether there is an official Anglican view on this subject. Historical theology like this is not intended to tell us what to believe. 'Historical theology is ministerial, not magisterial,' writes Gregg Allison, 'It does not possess the authority to determine doctrine and practice like the other disciplines [exegetical, biblical, and systematic theology], but it still has a very important role to play as an aid to the other three.'[1]

3.1. From the Fathers to the Reformation

The extent of God's intentions in sending his son to die did not become a major area of dispute across the churches until after the Reformation. Late sixteenth century theologians were not, however, the first to ponder the issue as it arose from a study of the biblical data.

As we noted previously, the early biblical scholar Origen (185-254) considered Christ to have died for humanity, the fallen angels, and even stars. 'It would surely be absurd,' he claimed, 'to say that [Christ] tasted death for human sins and not for any other being besides man which had fallen into sin, as for example for the stars.'[2] He has often been cited as a major figure in the development of universal salvation, not just universal atonement. Bishop Ambrose (337-397), however, wrote that 'if Christ died for all, yet he suffered particularly (*specialiter*) for us, because he suffered for the church.'[3]

---

[1] G. Allison, *Historical Theology: An Introduction to Christian Doctrine* (Grand Rapids: Zondervan, 2011), p 33 echoing Jim Packer.

[2] See Schaff, *Ante-Nicene Fathers* (Peabody: Hendrickson, 1994), 9: pp 318-319 (Book 1 Section 40 of his commentary on John): Cf. his *De Principiis*, chapter 7.

[3] *Expositio Evangelii Secundum Lucam*, 6.25.

Jerome (345-420),[4] Augustine (354-430),[5] and Prosper of Aquitaine (390-455),[6] all wrestled with this and related issues, providing much of the theological and exegetical foundations for later thinking.

Augustine, for instance, when commenting on 1 Timothy 2:4 '[God] desires all people to be saved,' comments, 'we are to understand by "all people," the human race in all its varieties of rank and circumstances.' This was his preferred understanding of the text, although he adds, 'we may interpret it in any other way we please, as long as we are not compelled to believe that the omnipotent God has willed anything to be done which was not done.' In other words, no-one God wants to save can finally end up in hell. Augustine makes his core commitment to God's sovereignty clear, saying,

> when we hear and read in the sacred scriptures that he "wills all people to be saved," although we are certain that all people are not saved, we ought not however to restrict the omnipotent will of God on that account, but ought rather to understand the scripture, "who will have all people to be saved," as meaning that no one is saved unless God wills it... and that, therefore, we should ask him to will it, because if he will it, it must necessarily be done.[7]

Although he could refer to Christ as 'the Redeemer of all' (*Redemptor omnium*), Gregory the Great (540-604) also wrote of 'our Redeemer' that, 'The author of life handed himself over, even to death, for the life of the elect,' that is, those who imitate him and have him as their head.[8] He did not develop this thought in any great depth. The medieval monk, Gottschalk of Orbais (808-867), however, explicitly held to both double predestination and limited atonement, in a way

---

[4]   See Blacketer, 'Definite Atonement', p 308.
[5]   Blacketer, *ibid.*, pp 308-310 who is even more persuasive on this than W.R. Godfrey, 'Reformed Thought On The Extent Of The Atonement To 1618' in *Westminster Theological Journal* 37.2 (Winter 1974), pp 133-134. Cf. Thomas, *Extent*, pp 4-5. Hodge, *Systematic Theology*, 2: p 548 is perhaps too confident of Augustine's entire approval when he calls limited atonement 'the Augustinian doctrine'.
[6]   W.R. Godfrey, 'Reformed Thought', pp 135-136.
[7]   *Enchiridion*, 27, 103 (my translation).
[8]   Gregory the Great, *Homilies on the Prophet Ezekiel*, 1.2 in *Patrologia Latina* 76: p 804: 'pro electorum vita usque ad mortem se tradidit auctor vitae... Caput quippe omnium nostrum Redemptor noster est.'

that got him into trouble.[9] Gottschalk was imprisoned by the Archbishop of Rheims, an ecclesiastical bully who took a more semi-Pelagian view of predestination and redemption.[10] A great debate ensued between 849-860.[11] As Victor Genke comments, however, 'To a certain extent what bothered people was not so much in *what* actually Gottschalk taught, but *how* he did it. His behaviour patterns sometimes bordered on those of a sociopath.'[12] What Gottschalk taught though, was clearly related to Augustine and was a precursor of the Reformed doctrine of the cross.

Gottschalk said that Christ did not shed his blood for those who are not elect, 'nor was he in any way crucified for them.' Rather, 'he deigned to be the repairer and restorer of all the elect alone.'[13] Indeed, 'he who says... the Lord suffered in general for the salvation and redemption of all, that is, of both the elect and the reprobate, contradicts God the Father.' If these should cite 2 Peter 2:1 ('denying the Master who bought them'), Gottschalk replied that 'he bought them by the sacrament of baptism, but did not suffer the cross, undergo death, or shed his blood for them.'[14] There are, he says, ten ways in which scripture speaks of 'redemption.' One is by the grace of baptism, which redeems both elect and reprobate from past sins; but there is also a 'special redemption for the elect,' and them alone, by which they are redeemed from all sins, past, present, and future, and from eternal damnation.[15] So there is a common redemption in baptism, a temporal redemption from 'diabolical captivity,'[16] and this

---

[9] Blacketer, 'Definite Atonement', pp 310-311.

[10] See Hincmarus Rhemensis, *De Praedestinatione Dei et Libero Arbitrio Posterior Dissertatio Adversus Gothescalcum et caeteros Praedestinatianos* in *Patrologia Latina* 125, esp. chapter 33 concerning how '*generaliter Christum fuisse passum pro omnibus*', 'Christ suffered generally for all.'

[11] On Gottschalk, who is better known on the continent, see D.E. Nineham, 'Gottschalk of Orbais: Reactionary or Precursor of the Reformation?' in *Journal of Ecclesiastical History* 40 (1989), pp 1-18 especially p 5 where Nineham points out that some of Hincmar's apparent quotations from Augustine against Gottschalk were actually from the Arch-heretic Pelagius!

[12] Genke and Gumerlock, *Gottschalk*, p 62. See also pp 41-43 on his 'unusual manner.'

[13] *Reply to Rabanus Maurus*, 8.

[14] *Tome to Gislemar*, 2.

[15] See 'On Different Ways of Speaking About Redemption' in Genke and Gumerlock, *Gottschalk*, pp 156-158.

[16] *Tome to Gislemar*, 3.

is what 2 Peter 2:1 is referring to; but 'that redemption that has been produced by the blood of Christ's cross is proper to and special for the elect only.'[17] This alone is everlasting and eternal redemption.

Gottschalk insists that 'the good shepherd laid down his life for his sheep alone... the Lord suffered only for the elect... those who say that Christ suffered in general for all human beings, that is, in the same way for both the elect and the reprobate, are clearly refuted.' This for him was a vital truth: 'we most certainly believe, understand, and most firmly confess and assert unto death that the Lord suffered for the elect alone and redeemed them through the blood of his cross from absolutely all sins, that is, from past, present, and future ones.'[18]

As a forerunner of the later scholastics, Gottschalk also uses syllogisms to support his view of the atonement. We have already noted how he demonstrates the underlying logic of Romans 8:32 to be in favour of particular redemption. He also uses syllogisms based on Romans 5:8-10 and 2 Corinthians 5:19, as well as this:

- Christ redeemed us from curse of the Law, so we are blessed (Galatians 3:13);
- but the reprobate are accursed, not blessed (Matthew 25:41);
- therefore Christ did not redeem the reprobate from the curse of the law,
- nor did he become a curse for them.[19]

So his conclusion is clear:

> whether the enemies of the truth and friends of error, lies, and falsehood like it or not, Christ redeemed only his holy church and only the elect, that is, only his body and members, through the blood of the cross; he was certainly crucified only for them, and he undoubtedly suffered the death of the cross, which was the most disgraceful, ignominious, and shameful death of that time, only for them.[20]

---

[17] *On Predestination*, 6.
[18] *On Predestination*, 5-6.
[19] *Answers to Various Questions*, 6.
[20] *On Predestination*, 11.

Gottschalk was defended on double predestination by Ratramnus of Corbie (died c.870), and several others.[21] Indeed, as Timothy Roberts makes clear, 'the best respected theologians of the period tended to support Gottschalk's theories, while those who opposed him were either not noted by their contemporaries as theologians... or else were held in positive disregard.'[22] Unfortunately for him, Gottschalk fell into the hands of the latter, and was severely beaten and imprisoned for his views on predestination and limited atonement. Archbishop Hincmar and others attempted to defend their rather severe actions against the Saxon monk. In response, a supporter wrote that 'if the shallowness of that wretched monk is condemned, his temerity disapproved, his insolent talkativeness blamed, divine truth should not for that reason be denied... Absolutely everyone therefore not only deplores but also shudders at the unheard of and conscienceless brutality by which the wretched man was slashed to ribbons with murderous floggings.'[23]

Gottschalk's views were generally supported by prominent contemporary theologians such as Florus of Lyon, Remigius of Lyon, Prudentius of Troyes, and Lupus of Ferrieres. They escaped such harsh treatment and continued the debate. Lupus, for example, wrote in support of Gottschalk's views, agreeing that Christ 'took the form of a servant, so that he might shed blood for the world, though he did not say "to give his life a ransom for all," but "for many," that is, for those who are willing to believe.'[24] Remigius defended Gottschalk, who, it was said, taught concerning 1 Timothy 2:4 that, 'God does not will all men to be saved, but only those who are saved,' adding that 'Christ did not come to save all, or to suffer for all, but only on behalf

---

[21] Ratramnus is significant because his anti-realist doctrine of the Lord's Supper later strongly influenced the English Reformers, especially Nicholas Ridley and Thomas Cranmer. See G. McCracken (ed.), *Early Medieval Theology* (Louisville: Westminster, 1957), pp 109-147. His book on predestination does not address the issue of the atonement's relationship to election, though it supports Gottschalk's double predestination doctrine with scripture, a host of patristic quotations, and arguments from God's simplicity and immutability.

[22] T.R. Roberts, *A Translation and Critical Edition of Ratramnus of Corbie's De Predestinatione Dei* (Unpublished PhD thesis, University of Missouri-Columbia, 1977), pp 11-12.

[23] 'A Reply to the Three Letters,' in McCracken, *Early Medieval Theology*, pp 163, 169.

[24] Lupus Ferrariensis, *Epistola CXXVIII* in *Patrologia Latina* 119: p 604c-d.

of those who are saved by the mystery of his suffering.'[25] Remigius expounds this idea with a string of verses about Christ dying for his sheep, the many, his people, concluding with a note about how 'all' or 'whole world' in disputed verses must be understood in context.[26] On 1 Timothy 2:5-6, he points out that the 'all' for whom Christ gave himself a ransom must be the same people for whom Christ is mediator; and he is not a mediator or advocate for unbelievers but the faithful only.[27]

Moving on to Anselm of Canterbury (1033-1109), we do not find an extended treatment of this subject such as Gottschalk indulged in. However, Anselm did write in his famous book *Cur Deus Homo* (Why God became Man), 'To whom is it more fitting for him to assign the fruit and recompense (*fructum et retributionem*) of his death than those for whose salvation (*propter quos salvandos*), as the logic of truth has taught us, he made himself man?' The underlying assumption here seems to be that the incarnation was undertaken for a specific group of people (in the context, his family, those who imitate him), and it is they who most appropriately benefit from the application of the (infinitely precious) atonement and are forgiven their debts. The response of Anselm's interlocutor (who rejoiced in the name Boso) is illuminating: 'Nothing more reasonable, more sweet, more desirable can the world hear! I take such confidence from this that I cannot describe the joy with which my heart exults.'[28] The fact that Christ came with a definite intention for us and for our salvation was a source of joy and assurance.

---

[25] Remigius Lugdunensis, *De Tribus Epistolis Liber* in *Patrologia Latina* 121: p 988a-b: 'Christus non venit ut omnes salvaret, nec passus est pro omnibus, nisi solummodo pro his qui passionis ejus salvantur mysterio.'

[26] *Ibid., Caput XIV: De Morte Christi*, Col. 1010d-1012a.

[27] *Ibid., Caput XVI*, Col. 1014c-101015a. In chapter 18 he looks at how absurd it would be to say Christ died for the wicked who had been in hell for thousands of years already before he came. If he did not suffer for them, how can it be said that he was crucified for the salvation of those who will perish in their impiety *after* the cross? In chapter 19 he mentions the case of Judas, who could not be punished in hell if he shared in Christ's redemption. The conclusion in chapter 20 is that Christ died '*pro solis fidelibus*,' for the faithful alone. Responding to Rabanus in chapter 47 he also concludes that Christ came to help all the elect with the price of his blood, but did not come to help the reprobate.

[28] *Cur Deus Homo*, 2.19.

Peter Lombard (1100-1160), who always attempted to stick closely to Augustine in his presentation of Christian doctrine, provides us with the most famous and commonly accepted formula for summarising this doctrine. Christ, he said, 'offered himself on the altar of the cross not to the devil, but to the triune God, and he did so for all with regard to the sufficiency of the price, but only for the elect with regard to its efficacy, because he brought about salvation only for the predestined.[29] Later he discusses whether Christ loves and desires the salvation of all. Contrasting two manners of loving, that of the 'fatherland' and that 'of the way' he concludes that 'Christ loved the elect alone like himself and desired their salvation.' The ultimate reason for why some are not saved is not to do with their rejection of God 'on the way,' but with God's justice and will.[30]

Thomas Aquinas (1225-1274) was happy with Lombard's sufficiency-efficacy formula. He also taught several key elements of the later doctrine, restricting, for instance, the efficacy of Christ's satisfaction to the elect.[31] On Hebrews 9:28 he says, 'the death of Christ, even if it is sufficient for all, yet does not have efficacy except for those who are to be saved.'[32] As Francis Turretin says, 'Among the ancients, it appears that the universality of redemption [i.e. 'unlimited atonement', not universal salvation] was contended for by the Pelagians and Semipelagians,' and was not something distinctively affirmed by the orthodox.[33] That is not to say Aquinas and others held to limited atonement in the way that post-Reformation Protestants formulated it. They did not. Yet even if some of them may have been attracted to a form of what is later called hypothetical universalism, they clearly would not have had sympathy with the Arminian view.

---

[29] *Sententiae in IV Libris Distinctae* 3.20.5. There is now a good English translation of the whole of Lombard's *Sentences*; this quotation is from *The Sentences Book 3: On the Incarnation of the Word* trans. Giulio Silano (Toronto: Pontifical Institute of Mediaeval Studies, 2008), p 86.

[30] *Ibid.*, 132. *Sentences* 3.31.3.

[31] See L. Gatiss, 'Grace Tasted Death for All: Thomas Aquinas on Hebrews 2:9,' in *Tyndale Bulletin 62.2* (2012).

[32] Aquinas, *Commentary on the Epistle to the Hebrews* (South Bend, Indiana: St Augustine's Press, 2006), p 199. He also restricts the spiritually-saving efficacy of the cross to the faithful in his comments on 1 Timothy 4:10 in *Commentaries on St. Paul's Epistles to Timothy, Titus, and Philemon* (South Bend, Indiana: St Augustine's Press, 2007), p 56.

[33] See Turretin, *Institutes* 2.14.XIV.ii on p 455.

So this subject of the intent of the atonement was by no means raised for the first time in the seventeenth century. We will look more at Calvin's view below, but the sixteenth century reformers were not unaware of the distinctions that could be made in terms of the extent of the atonement. Their medieval predecessors Wycliffe and Hus had held to definite atonement, according to one study,[34] and so perhaps played a part in passing it on. When commenting on Romans 8:28-39, the great Martin Luther himself wrote that verses in scripture about the salvation of all (such as 1 Timothy 2:4), 'must be understood only with respect to the elect... Christ did not die for absolutely all.'[35]

3.2. John Calvin's view

We come now to look at the debate which has raged over what John Calvin thought on this issue. This is of particular relevance to those who see him as the fountainhead of Reformed theology in its 'pristine spirit'[36] and claim to be in that same tradition today. Given Calvin's great stature and reputation amongst Protestant and particularly Reformed theologians in the seventeenth century, it is no wonder that both sides in the debate over the extent of the atonement looked to his writings for support. This had already begun to happen in the seventeenth century,[37] but claiming Calvin for support has also been a more modern occupation. People have been keen to discover what Calvin might have said had he been at the Synod of Dort (more than 50 years after he died) when the so-called 'five points of Calvinism' were defined. Yet, as Richard Muller writes,

> Virtually all these studies exist primarily for the sake of enlisting Calvin's support in the establishment or justification

---

[34] J.H. Rainbow, *The Will of God and the Cross: An Historical and Theological Study of John Calvin's Doctrine of Limited Redemption* (Allison Park: Pickwick, 1990), pp 34-46.

[35] *Luther: Lectures on Romans* (Philadelphia: Westminster, 1961), p 252 (*scholia in Romans* 8, II). Cf. T. George, *Theology of the Reformers*, p 77. Luther made a similar point, citing Chrysostom in support, on 'the many' in Hebrews 9:28; *Luther: Early Theological Works* (Louisville: Westminster, 1962), p 187.

[36] To use Blacketer's phrase from 'Definite Atonement', p 305.

[37] See, classically, Moses Amyraut's, *Defense de la Doctrine de Calvin* (Saumur, 1644). Cf. B.G. Armstrong, *Calvinism and the Amyraut Heresy*, pp 99-100.

of a contemporary theological program – and their method consists in the gathering of comments from various of Calvin's works for the sake of reframing them into a full-scale doctrine either of limited, or universal, or, indeed, hypothetically universal atonement.[38]

One example of this is the 'Calvin against the Calvinists' school of thought which pits the great Genevan reformer against those who claimed to be his theological successors.[39] Epitomising this view, R.T. Kendall's *Calvin and English Calvinism* avers that Calvin was not himself a Calvinist on the point of limited atonement.[40] Kendall's position is that Calvin limited the extent of the *intercession* of Christ rather than his work of atonement.[41] Indeed, he claims that 'Fundamental to the doctrine of faith in John Calvin (1509-64) is his belief that Christ died indiscriminately for all men.'[42]

To say the least, it is bold to make a highly disputed point so essential to the wider structure of Calvin's theology. It is especially courageous since Calvin seems never to have directly addressed the question as a live issue in his day. Kendall assures us, however, that although Arminius differs with Calvin about the extent of Christ's intercession, 'Arminius and Calvin have in common the belief that Christ died for all.'[43] The idea of universal atonement was obvious for

---

[38] R.A. Muller, *The Unaccommodated Calvin: Studies in the Foundation of a Theological Tradition* (Oxford: Oxford University Press, 2000), p 6.

[39] See the eponymous article by B. Hall, 'Calvin against the Calvinists,' in G.E. Duffield, *John Calvin* (Grand Rapids: Eerdmans, 1966), pp 19-37. Earlier, Paul Van Duren had denied that Calvin taught limited atonement but without going further to pit Calvin against the Calvinists. See Van Duren, *Christ in our Place: The Substitutionary Character of Calvin's Doctrine of Reconciliation* (Edinburgh: Oliver and Boyd, 1957) and the unfavourable review of this by J. Murray in *Collected Writings of John Murray* (Edinburgh: Banner of Truth, 1982), 4: pp 310-314.

[40] Kendall, *Calvin and English Calvinism*, p viii puts it succinctly when he says, 'As for Calvin's own "Calvinism", I would give him four-and-a-half points out of the traditional five.'

[41] Kendall, *ibid.*, vii and pp 13-16. Interestingly J.C. Ryle says the same thing: 'The atonement was made for all the world, though it is applied to and enjoyed by none but believers – Christ's intercession is the peculiar privilege of His people.' *Expository Thoughts on John*, I: p 62.

[42] Kendall, *Calvin and English Calvinism*, p 13.

[43] Kendall, *ibid.*, p 149.

Calvin because of the passages of scripture which speak of Christ dying for 'all' or for 'the world'; he did not need to expound this at length because it was so clear from the Bible itself, Kendall declares. In his commentaries (we are told), 'he generally leaves verses like these alone, but never does he explain, for example, that "all" does not mean *all* or "world" does not mean *world*.'[44]

This is a highly dubious claim. In a later reprint of his book, Kendall adds an appendix 'to let the unbiased reader have a wider look at some of Calvin's statements regarding the extent of the atonement.' Strangely, however, he omits any quotations from Calvin's commentary on 1 Timothy 2:1-6 (a classic passage in limited atonement discussions). Looking up Calvin's comments on this, we find that he is very careful to say, on more than one occasion, that 'all' does not mean 'all without exception'. Indeed, on 1 Timothy 2:5 Calvin insists that, 'The universal term *all* must always be referred to classes of men, and not to persons.'[45] Kendall does however quote Calvin's comments on 1 John 2:2 where the Reformer explains that the view which sees 'the world' in that verse as including even the reprobate (as Kendall would like it to) is a fanatical dream and a monstrous absurdity! What is the 'unbiased reader' to make of this?

Furthermore, Kendall asserts that the puritans who taught limited atonement and professed to be following in his tracks actually ended up opposing and repudiating Calvin's theology and the basic thrust of Reformation teaching. Their theology led to 'endless introspection, the constant checking of the spiritual pulse for the right "effects", and, possibly, legalism.'[46] Moreover, it was fatally

---

[44]   Kendall, *ibid.*, p 13 n2. Some passages in Calvin's writings which contain the vocabulary of Christ dying or satisfying for 'the sins of the world' (often alluding to John 1:29) are conveniently collected at www.calvinandcalvinism.com. They are often employed to demonstrate his 'ubiquitous universalism' as in A.C. Clifford, 'Calvin & Calvinism: Amyraut et al' in A.C. Clifford (ed.), *John Calvin: A Reformation Affirmation (Amyraldian Association 2009 Conference Report)* (Oswestry: Charenton Reformed Publishing, 2011), pp 37-79.

[45]   J. Calvin, *Calvin's Commentaries Volume XXI* (Grand Rapids: Baker, 1993), p 57.

[46]   Kendall, *ibid.*, p 208. It is worth noting that Moses Amyraut, who held to a form of hypothetical universalism that would seem otherwise to please Kendall, was actually quite content with 'feeling the pulse of the soul' for assurance and consolation. See his *Brief Traitté de la Predestination... Nouvelle Edition reveuë & corrigée* (Saumur, 1658), pp 155-156 and Lum, *Brief Treatise on Predestination*, 91 n1.

flawed by 'the crypto-Arminian doctrine of faith' that he says pervaded the theology of the Westminster Assembly and divines.[47] Thus Calvin's work was undone by those calling themselves Calvinists. The root of this error was, apparently, the explicit teaching on limited atonement of Calvin's successor at Geneva, Theodore Beza.[48] Others also identify Beza as 'the chief culprit in this move away from the scriptural roots of the reformation.'[49] Roger Nicole's withering response to this aspect of Kendall's thesis is to ask, 'can we really accept that his influence was so very far-reaching that he practically single-handedly reversed the whole trend in Reformed circles, putting himself at loggerheads not only with Calvin, but as it is alleged, with scripture itself, and this without producing any major work centering on this topic? Somehow a lot more light should be shed on this area before such an unlikely development can be assumed to have taken place.'[50]

In answer to Kendall, Paul Helm's *Calvin and the Calvinists* is a classic response.[51] He argues 'both that his account of Calvin is inaccurate and that he provides a wildly exaggerated picture of Puritanism.'[52] He points out that Kendall's view that Calvin limits the intercession of Christ is so novel as to have never been noticed by any other citable reader of Calvin. Though it is technically possible that no-one prior to Kendall writing his doctorate had spotted something of absolutely crucial importance to Calvin (as Kendall alleges), it is not particularly plausible.[53] It is not particularly biblical to separate atonement and intercession either. There are some for whom Christ explicitly does not pray (John 17:9), and it seems that those for whom

---

[47] *ibid.*, p 209.

[48] *ibid.*, p 38.

[49] Blacketer, 'Definite Atonement', p 306. See p 307 n8 for details of studies which effectively redraw this distorted picture of Beza as the corrupter of Calvinism.

[50] R. Nicole, 'John Calvin's View of the Extent of the Atonement' in *Westminster Theological Journal* 47.2 (Fall 1985), pp 224-225.

[51] The basic controversy about the continuity of later Calvinism with Calvin pre-dates the Kendall-Helm exchange. See for instance the opposing views of R. Nicole, 'Moyse Amyraut (1596-1664) and the Controversy on Universal Grace, First Phase (1634-1637)' (PhD Dissertation: Harvard, 1966) and Armstrong, *Calvinism and the Amyraut Heresy.*

[52] P. Helm, *Calvin and the Calvinists* (Edinburgh: Banner of Truth, [1982] 1998), p 10.

[53] *Ibid.*, pp 36-38.

he died are the same group as those for whom he intercedes (Romans 8:34).[54]

Helm also demonstrates that although Calvin does not speak of 'limited atonement' in those words he does teach key elements of the doctrine. For example, Calvin writes against Pighius that, 'Christ was *so* ordained the Saviour of the world, as that he might save those that were given unto him by the Father *out of* the whole world.'[55] As Helm concludes, 'Calvin teaches that the death of Christ actually remitted sin, that such remission was for the elect, and that Christ intended to die for the elect.'[56]

Helm very effectively challenges Kendall's exegesis of Calvin's commentaries. To make them favour Kendall's view they must be divorced from their context and somewhat twisted.[57] As John Murray was quick to argue, 'if there are any texts which offered Calvin the opportunity to set forth the doctrine of universal atonement they are 1 John 2:2 and 1 Timothy 2:4,6'[58] and yet it is precisely when commenting on those texts that Calvin is so careful to say that 'the whole world' for which Christ's propitiation was offered 'does not include all the reprobate.'[59] When Calvin says of the disputed clause of 1 John 2:2, 'I pass by the dotages of the fanatics, who under this pretence extend salvation to all the reprobate, and therefore to Satan himself,' he assumes that if the expiation or propitiation is made for someone then their *salvation* is assured. With that linkage he could not have held to unlimited atonement without being a universalist (unless he was inconsistent with his own exegesis, which – we must confess – is always a possibility for a mere mortal).[60]

Elsewhere Calvin says that the 'all' whom God wishes to save and for whom Christ has paid the ransom 'must always be referred to

---

[54] Gottschalk, *On Predestination*, 5, also links these two texts to make this point.

[55] *A Treatise on the Eternal Predestination of God in Calvin's Calvinism* (London: Sovereign Grace Union, 1927), p 94 (my emphasis).

[56] Helm, *Calvin and the Calvinists*, p 30.

[57] *Ibid.*, pp 38-46.

[58] Murray, *Collected Writings of John Murray*, 4: p 313.

[59] *Calvin's Commentaries Volume XXII* (Grand Rapids: Baker, 1993), p 173 (on 1 John 2:2).

[60] Likewise, we should have no problem admitting that Calvin may have misspoken, changed his mind, been unclear, or got something wrong. See James 3:2.

classes of men, and not to persons.' He clarifies further by saying, 'the Apostle simply means, that there is no people and no rank in the world that is excluded from salvation; because God wishes that the gospel should be proclaimed to all without exception... God invites all equally to partake of salvation. But the present discourse relates to classes of men, and not to individual persons; for his sole object is, to include in this number princes and foreign nations.'[61] Hence I think Helm is right to conclude that 'Kendall has often been driven to mangle and distort the evidence and confidently to put forward novel views for which there is little or no support.'[62] It is possible, but not especially profitable, to play proof-text ping-pong with Calvin on these issues, however, and it seems to me that in his sermons especially Calvin was somewhat looser in his phraseology than in his more considered writing.[63] Those who dislike definite atonement sometimes claim that although the Bible says Christ died for the church or for his sheep, it does not add a negative statement such as 'and he did not die for the goats.' So, in the same vein, it might also be pointed out that although thought-provoking lists may be compiled of places where Calvin refers to Christ as 'Redeemer of the world' or as suffering 'for mankind' or 'for all', there appears to be no place where he follows this with an unambiguous negation, such as 'and he did not die just for the elect.' So this debate, like that over scripture, must look beyond mere proof-texts.

Amongst Barthian reinterpreters of Calvin the issue of limited atonement arises as part of a consideration of Christ's incarnational union with humanity. Did he enter into a redemptive union with all humanity simply by virtue of taking human flesh, or was that union non-redemptive in and of itself? As Kevin Kennedy puts it: 'Since Christ shared this common fraternal union with all of humanity, in Calvin's mind, Christ's death could have been nothing

---

[61] *Calvin's Commentaries Volume XXI* (Grand Rapids: Baker, 1993), p 57 (on 1 Timothy 2:4). Cf. pp 54-55.

[62] Helm, *Calvin and the Calvinists*, p 80.

[63] It is worth bearing in mind that he did not regularly check the text of sermons (which were published by those who scribbled down his words as best they could) prior to their publication.

other than a death for all of humanity.'[64] How a person can be incarnationally united to Christ and yet still end up lost is a question that 'has bedevilled the Barthian *schema* and led to regular charges of universalism.'[65] Certainly the incarnation was a prerequisite for the atonement,[66] which Calvin spends some time defending in *Institutes* II.xii. Yet a recent study of Calvin's correspondence with Vermigli,[67] and my own study of Calvin's work on Ephesians,[68] make very clear that he certainly did not consider incarnational union to be salvific. As Bavinck says, 'if the incarnation had itself effected the reconciliation and union of God and man, there would have been no place for a living, and especially not for a dying, of the Lord Jesus.'[69] Calvin would certainly agree. Preaching on Ephesians 5:30-31 he said that Christ takes our flesh and bones in the incarnation so that by the special power of the Spirit we, the church, might become 'bone of his bones and flesh of his flesh.' He unites himself with humanity physically, in order to redeem his elect spiritually.[70]

Sometimes quoted is this statement by Calvin where he certainly seems to assume a doctrine of limited atonement, in the context of his sacramental polemics:

> ...the first thing to be explained is how Christ is present with unbelievers, as being the spiritual food of souls and, in short, the life and salvation of the world... I should like to know how

---

[64] K.D. Kennedy, *Union with Christ and the Extent of the Atonement* (New York: Peter Lang, 2002), p 149. A *spiritual* union is necessary on top of this in order for the benefits of Christ's work to be appropriated; the incarnational union is not of itself salvific on Kennedy's scheme. But see J.B. Torrance, 'The Incarnation and "Limited Atonement"', pp 32-40 and T. Hart, 'Humankind in Christ', especially pp 79-84. Kennedy acknowledges an affinity to Hart on p 14.

[65] A.T.B. McGowan, 'Was Westminster Calvinist?' in L. Quigley (ed.), *Reformed Theology in Contemporary Perspective: Westminster: Yesterday, Today – and Tomorrow?* (Edinburgh: Rutherford House, 2006), p 55.

[66] See R.A. Peterson, *Calvin and the Atonement* (Fearn: Mentor, 1999), pp 25-44.

[67] M.A. Garcia, *Life in Christ: Union with Christ and Twofold Grace in Calvin's Theology* (Carlisle: Paternoster, 2008), pp 191-193.

[68] Lee Gatiss, 'The Inexhaustible Fountain of All Good Things: Union with Christ in Calvin on Ephesians,' in *Themelios* 34.2 (July 2009), pp 204-206.

[69] H. Bavinck, *Our Reasonable Faith: A Survey of Christian Doctrine* (Grand Rapids: Eerdmans, 1956), p 331.

[70] J. Calvin, *Sermons on the Epistle to the Ephesians* (Edinburgh: Banner of Truth, 1973), p 602.

the wicked can eat the flesh of Christ which was *not crucified for them*, and how they can drink the blood which was *not shed to expiate their sins?*[71]

This appears to restrict the crucifixion and expiation of Christ, excluding 'the wicked' from the 'salvation of the world.' Some may quibble at this,[72] and perhaps we ought not to rest too much upon it. In my view, however, it is safe to conclude with Mark Garcia that 'Calvin's line of thinking bears a more positive relationship to the later terminology of a limited atonement than some have wished to perceive.'[73] It is certainly correct to affirm with Blocher that, 'Calvin gives no hint of hypothetical universalism when commenting on Amyraldian proof-texts.'[74] What the Reformer of Geneva might have said at Dort must remain a mystery and somewhat ambiguous, in that he can be selectively quoted on either side of the debate. Putting all his statements together into a satisfying, coherent whole is genuinely challenging.[75] Given what was said above about the pre-history of the debate, Calvin had probably at least encountered the idea of limited atonement in his lifetime,[76] and it is at least possible that he deliberately avoided taking a view in a more explicit discussion of it. Yet I do not think his underlying sympathies (given

---

[71]   (my emphasis) J. Calvin, 'Clear Explanation of Sound Doctrine concerning the True Partaking of the Flesh and Blood of Christ in the Holy Supper in order to Dissipate the Mists of Tileman Heshusius,' in *Treatises on the Sacraments* (Fearn: Christian Heritage, 2002), p 527 (*De Vera Participatione*, CO 9.484).

[72]   Garcia notes that a small degree of uncertainty must remain because we do not have access to Heshusius's original to which Calvin is responding. See also the slight hesitations of an otherwise positive H. Blocher, 'The Atonement in John Calvin's Theology', pp 280-281 (footnote 8) and the less convincing cavils of Thomas, *Extent*, p 39 n58. P.L. Rouwendal, 'Calvin's Forgotten Classical Position on the Extent of the Atonement: About Sufficiency, Efficiency, and Anachronism,' in *Westminster Theological Journal* 70.2 (Fall 2008), pp 330-331 also questions the use of this passage, though unconvincingly in my view.

[73]   *Life in Christ*, p 192.

[74]   H. Blocher, 'The Atonement in John Calvin's Theology', p 280.

[75]   Although he is probably onto something in pointing out the tendentious nature of some readings, the recent stimulating attempt at presenting Calvin's position by Rouwendal, 'Calvin's Forgotten Classical Position' is no more satisfying itself, and relies perhaps too heavily on an incoherent taxonomy and on Voetius, without adequately analysing the 'universalist' passages he cites.

[76]   Thomas, *Extent*, 12 makes a good case for believing Calvin was at least aware of the issue.

his wider doctrinal commitments) would have been with the Arminians, or later with the Amyraldians or Barthians.[77] We can probably go further and agree on the 'Calvin against the Calvinists' issue with Stephen Holmes that, 'there is no fundamental divergence between Calvin and the later tradition on the question of limited atonement; the later teaching is no more than a making explicit of what was implicit in Calvin's theology.'[78]

Whether this is as important as the amount of ink spilled on the question would suggest is uncertain. The Reformed tradition was not, of course, the brainchild of just one man, even a giant like Calvin. Others stood in that same theological current, and were unambiguous about definite atonement. It is certainly noteworthy that Calvin never seems to have taken issue publicly with them about this.[79] Acknowledging that it is a 'fallacious assumption that Calvin's thought should be the sole criterion of what is genuinely Reformed'[80] should facilitate a more historically accurate and less emotionally weighted assessment of Calvin's doctrine. Yet Richard Muller's conclusion on the 'Calvin vs. the Calvinists' battle is the most persuasive: 'If there is a difference between "Calvin" and the "Calvinists," on this point,' he writes, 'it is simply that, in the case of the Reformers, one must make a little effort to "connect the dots," whereas the Reformed orthodox made sure, against various doctrinal adversaries, that the picture was presented in full.'[81]

3.3. The Synod of Dort

The question of whether Christ died effectually for the elect alone or for everyone was certainly discussed in the sixteenth century. Robert Some (1542–1609), Master of Peterhouse in Cambridge, published a

---

[77] Cf. the similar conclusion of McGowan in 'Was Westminster Calvinist?', p 62. Pace A.N.S. Lane, A Reader's Guide to Calvin's Institutes (Grand Rapids: Baker, 2009), p 98 who thinks that the thrust of Calvin's teaching 'points to universal rather than limited atonement.'

[78] S.R. Holmes, Listening to the Past: The Place of Tradition in Theology (Carlisle: Paternoster, 2002), p 80.

[79] As Reymond, A New Systematic Theology, p 672 n3 observes.

[80] Blacketer, 'Definite Atonement', pp 307, 315-317.

[81] Muller, After Calvin: Studies in the Development of a Theological Tradition (Oxford: Oxford University Press, 2003), p 15.

brief tract on the subject in 1596. In response to high-profile challenges to the Reformed orthodoxy then current in the Church of England, he presented eight reasons for limiting the atonement to the elect, all taken from scripture, and answered several common objections to it.[82]

The issue became a major dividing issue, however, in the early seventeenth century. After the death of Arminius in 1609, forty-six of his followers in the Netherlands issued their 'Remonstrance' or protest against the Calvinist orthodoxy of the great majority of their fellow ministers. They summarised their creed under five points concerning predestination, the atonement, faith, grace, and perseverance.[83] Point two of the Remonstrance said,

> Jesus Christ, the Saviour of the world, died for all men and for every man, so that he has obtained for them all, by his death on the cross, redemption and the forgiveness of sins; yet that no-one actually enjoys this forgiveness of sins except the believer, according to the word of the Gospel (John 3:16): "God so loved the world that he gave his only-begotten Son, that whoever believes in him should not perish, but have everlasting life." And in 1 John 2:2: "And he is the propitiation for our sins, and not for ours only, but also for the sins of the whole world."[84]

This expresses Arminius' own views on the subject, found especially in a tract he wrote against William Perkins, a famous Cambridge Puritan.[85] A Counter-Remonstrance was issued by Calvinists and a conference was held in 1611 between the two parties but with no

---

[82] R. Some, *Three Questions, Godly, and Plainly, and Briefly Handled... III. Christ died effectually for the Elect alone: therfore not for every severall man* (Cambridge, 1596), pp 20-30. The texts that he employs are Matthew 1:21; John 10:15, 26, 17:9; Hebrews 7:25; Romans 8:33-34; 1 John 2:1-2; Matthew 26:28; Revelation 5:9; Romans 5:19; Hebrews 9:28; Colossians 1:14; John 11:49-52.

[83] These were probably suggested by a letter of Hincmar, the leader of the Synod of Chiercy (853), in which he condemned the doctrine of Gottschalk. See S. Strehle, 'The Extent of the Atonement and the Synod of Dort,' in *Westminster Theological Journal* 51.1 (Spring 1989), p 2 for more details.

[84] Text in G. Bray (ed.), *Documents of the English Reformation* (Cambridge: James Clarke & Co, 1994), p 454. Cf. Schaff, *The Creeds of Christendom* (Grand Rapids: Baker, 2000), 3: p 546.

[85] *Writings*, 3:345ff and 1: pp 316-317.

agreement reached.[86]   Then in 1618 after much controversy and preparation, the National Synod of Dort was convened to respond to the Arminian points. It is important to note that the famous 'Five Points of Calvinism' were therefore framed in a polemical context against the original 'Five Points of Arminianism.'[87]

The nature of the five points as responses should warn us, as Alan Sell puts it 'against thinking that they represent the *sum* of Calvinism.'[88] Reformed theology is also committed to the five Reformation *solas* (God's glory alone, scripture alone, Christ alone, grace alone, faith alone) to distinguish it from Roman Catholicism, for example. It has a view of the sacraments which distinguishes it from Lutheranism and a firm belief in the Trinity which sets it apart from various Unitarian sects. All of these commitments, some may argue, are of equal or greater significance than limited atonement (although that is certainly not to say it is unimportant).[89]

As Schaff notes, Dort was 'the only Synod of a quasi-œcumenical character in the history of the Reformed Churches' since delegates from several other countries were invited to attend with voting rights.[90] Their rejection of Arminianism was, we might say, predestined, because straightforwardly Arminian delegates were not permitted to vote, although they were allowed to speak their mind, and their views had a full hearing. The Synod was far from monochrome, with various shades of opinion expressed on several issues, not least on the atonement. Dissent from the majority view was certainly permitted, and one delegate even challenged another to

---

[86] See Schaff, *Creeds*, 1: pp 509-519.

[87] For more on the historical background, theology, exegesis, and aftermath of Dort, see Lee Gatiss, 'The Synod of Dort and Definite Atonement' in the edited volume *From Heaven He Came and Sought Her: Definite Atonement in Historical, Biblical, Theological & Pastoral Perspective* (Crossway, forthcoming).

[88] A.P.F. Sell, *The Great Debate: Calvinism, Arminianism and Salvation* (Eugene: Wipf and Stock, 1998), p 14.

[89] See further R.A. Muller, 'How Many Points?' in *Calvin Theological Journal* 28 (1993), pp 425-433 on the consequences of neglecting the wider doctrinal commitments of Reformed theology.

[90] Schaff, *Creeds*, 1: p 514.

a duel during the debates because of a disagreement! Sadly, passions often run high when definite atonement is discussed.[91]

This means that the final agreed statement was a consensus document which, especially on this doctrine, left several questions unanswered.[92] For instance, G.M. Thomas states that 'an explicit link between infinite sufficiency and indiscriminate preaching is avoided... [and] no explanation is offered as to how the sufficiency of Christ's death relates to the non-elect... As a result of the biggest disagreement of the Synod, it was impossible to find an acceptable way of relating universal and particular aspects of the atonement in the final document.'[93] Space was left for different Reformed churches to fill in such gaps in their own distinctive ways while preserving a clear framework of consensus against the Arminian position. Nor are the Canons of Dort as tightly logical and neat as some would like to claim since in them there is, 'no attempt to resolve the apparent contradiction between the assertion of universal sufficiency, preaching and inexcusability, on the one hand, and limited saving will and efficacy on the other.'[94]

The best way to grasp the seminal teaching of this crucial Synod, is to walk through the agreed statements of doctrine, or Canons. These are so important in the history of the doctrine we are examining that it is worth tip-toeing carefully through these particular tulips. The Canons were published in English fairly soon after the Synod itself,[95] and are also available in various modern translations.[96]

---

[91] John Hales was chaplain to the British Ambassador to the Netherlands at the time of the Synod. In a sermon against duelling preached at the Hague and recorded in *Golden Remains of the Ever Memorable Mr. John Hales* (London, 1673), i. p 71, he inveighs against 'an over-promptness in many young men, who desire to be counted men of valour and resolution, upon every sleight occasion to raise a quarrel, and admit of no other means of composing and ending it, but by sword and single combat.' Nowadays blogs are perhaps their weapon of choice.

[92] See Milton's comments in *The British Delegation*, pp 295-296 that 'The drawing up of the canons was a complex and acrimonious affair' which took three weeks.

[93] Thomas, *Extent*, p 133.

[94] *Ibid.*, p 133.

[95] *The Judgement of the Synode Holden at Dort, Concerning the Five Articles* (London, 1619). This is reproduced in Milton, *The British Delegation*, pp 297-321.

What follows is my own new translation of the agreed text on this 'Second Head of Doctrine,' with comments interspersed to help expound the significance of each Article.[97]

Second Head of Doctrine

The death of Christ and the redemption of people by it

> 1. *God is not only supremely merciful, but also supremely just. And his justice requires (as he himself has revealed in his word) that our sins committed against his infinite majesty should be punished, not only with temporal but also with eternal punishments, in both soul and body; which punishment we cannot escape, unless satisfaction is made to the justice of God.*

The Articles begin with the need for atonement. In a statement of God's so-called 'simplicity' and 'perfection,' the Reformed, along with patristic and medieval orthodoxy, do not say either that 'Law wins' or that 'Love wins' but that God's attributes should not be pitted against each other. As far back as Ulrich Zwingli (1484-1531), the Reformed tradition had made it clear that, 'God clothed his Son in the frailty of our flesh in order that we might see that his grace and mercy are no less supreme than his holiness and justice.'[98] Because he is both supremely just and supremely merciful, he cannot merely save sinners, but must punish sin. As usual, the Canons begin not by engaging immediately in controversy but with 'a statement of

---

[96] E.g. P. Schaff, *The Creeds of Christendom*, 3: pp 550-577 (Latin) and 3: pp 581-597 (English) and G.L. Bray, *Documents of the English Reformation* (Cambridge: James Clarke, 1994), pp 453-478. Most helpfully, P.Y. De Jong, *Crisis in the Reformed Churches: Essays in Commemoration of the Great Synod of Dort, 1618-1619* (Grand Rapids: Reformed Fellowship, 1968), pp 269-305 includes a translation of the *rejectio errorum* (rejection of errors), which others often omit.

[97] The translation was made directly from the authoritative Latin edition in *Acta Synodi Nationalis... Dordrechti Habitae* (Leiden, 1620), 1: pp 241-271. The suggestions of A.A. Hoekema, 'Needed: A New Translation of the Canons of Dort,' *Calvin Theological Journal* 3.1 (1968) and 'A New English Translation of the Canons of Dort,' *Calvin Theological Journal* 3.2 (1968) are valuable, although I disagree with his translation in several places for various reasons, and unfortunately he did not translate the *rejectio errorum*.

[98] *An Exposition of the Faith* in G. Bromiley (ed.), *Zwingli and Bullinger* (London: SCM, 1953), p 250.

Christian doctrine on which Roman Catholics, Lutherans, and the Reformed would all agree,' and working out from there to more Reformed statements. The Canons therefore, 'seek to demonstrate that these Reformed distinctives are the proper and necessary result of taking catholic doctrine seriously and faithfully.'[99]

> 2. *Since, however, we are unable to make that satisfaction ourselves, or to free ourselves from the wrath of God, God, in his infinite mercy, has given us as a Surety his only begotten Son, who, to make satisfaction for us, was made sin and became a curse on the cross for us and in our place.*

This is a classic statement of penal substitutionary atonement. Christ bore the eternal punishments (*æternis pœnis*) that we deserved for our sins. He did so 'for us' (*pro nobis*) and vicariously, 'in our place' (*vice nostra*).[100] Note that the problem we face is not our sin, or the mess it makes of our lives and the world, but the wrath of God against it. The Article alludes to both 2 Corinthians 5:21 and Galatians 3:13.

> 3. *This death of the Son of God is the only and most perfect sacrifice and satisfaction for sins, and is of infinite value and worth, abundantly sufficient to expiate the sins of the whole world.*

This makes it clear that no other satisfaction is needed except the death of Christ, in distinction from Roman Catholic theology. It also echoes the Lombardian formula that the death of Christ was 'sufficient for all' and infinitely precious.

> 4. *This death, therefore, is of such great value and worth because the person who submitted to it was not only truly man and*

---

[99] W. Robert Godfrey, 'Popular and Catholic: The *Modus Docendi* of the Canons of Dordt,' in Goudriaan and Frieburg, *Revisiting the Synod of Dordt*, p 258. He also makes the excellent point (p 260) that the academics at Dordt were pastors too, presenting a pastorally sensitive theology in touch with the wider 'catholic' tradition, and at a popular not scholarly level. 'While dialectic had triumphed in the schools,' he concludes, 'the Synod spoke the rhetorical language of the Reformers to the church. The *modus docendi* of the Synod of Dordt continued the work of the Reformation.'

[100] Van Genderen and Velema, *Concise Reformed Dogmatics*, p 526 point out that on the Remonstrant view Christ's death 'was for our sake and to our benefit, but not in our stead.' Hence the careful Dortian language here.

> *perfectly holy, but also the only-begotten Son of God, of the same eternal and infinite being with the Father and the Holy Spirit, which it was necessary for our Saviour to be; and, further, because his death was accompanied with a sense of the wrath and curse we deserved for our sins.*

Arminian declarations about the sufficiency of the cross usually spoke of it as intentionally sufficient or designed to be sufficient by God's eternal will. The Canons keep the language of intention to the second half of the Lombardian sufficient-efficient formula and make no link between the sufficiency of the cross and divine intention, perhaps to allow Reformed theologians with different views on this thorny issue space to disagree. They link sufficiency with the person of Christ himself, but do not say if this sufficiency has an effect on humanity (making it saveable) or not. Interestingly, they link the infinite worth of Jesus' death to both his divine nature *and* his perfect humanity and obedience, in an echo of *Heidelberg Catechism* 15-18, which was one of the Dutch Church's official doctrinal statements. This contrasts with Lutheran theology which generally links the intrinsic worth of Christ's death to his deity alone.[101]

> 5. *Moreover, the promise of the gospel is that whoever believes in Christ crucified shall not perish, but have eternal life. This promise ought to be declared and published promiscuously and without distinction, to all nations and people to whom God, according to his good pleasure, sends the gospel, together with the command to repent and believe.*

The question of the precise relationship between the sufficiency of the sacrifice and the universal offer of the gospel is not settled here (the connective *caeterum*, 'moreover' is deliberately not as strong as *ergo*, 'therefore'). Yet it is clear that Synod of Dort Calvinism thinks the gospel should be 'promiscuously' and indiscriminately proclaimed. Whoever repents and believes in Christ is saved (echoing John 3:16), although it is not said that unbelievers must believe *that* Christ died for them (which the Arminians complained would be inconsistent), only that they should believe in the crucified Christ.

---

[101] Scaer, 'Atonement in Lutheran Theology,' p 181.

> 6. *But although many who are called by the gospel do not repent nor believe in Christ, but perish in unbelief, this is not because of any defect in the sacrifice offered by Christ upon the cross, or indeed any insufficiency in it, but is their own particular fault.*

Jesus did not fail, or do anything wrong. No-one can point to any defect in his work and blame that for their condemnation on the Last Day. We are the authors of our own downfall if we refuse to repent and believe. It is important to stress this, because some people accuse Calvinists of making God the author of sin, or of leaving it open for unbelievers to blame God for their own rebellion 'because Jesus didn't die for me.' The Canons of Dort decisively reject this idea.

> 7. *But on the other hand, as many as truly believe, and are by the death of Christ freed and saved from sin and destruction, obtain this benefit solely by the grace of God (which he owes to no-one) given to them in Christ from eternity.*

If we perish it is our own fault; but if we live it is God's doing. He does not have to save anybody. If he saves anyone it is entirely by his unmerited grace.

> 8. *For this was the most free purpose and most gracious will and intention of God the Father, that the life-giving and saving efficacy of the most precious death of his Son should extend to all the elect, for bestowing upon them alone justifying faith, thereby to bring them unfailingly to salvation; that is, God willed that Christ through the blood of the cross (by which he confirmed the new covenant) should effectually redeem out of every people, tribe, nation, and language, all those, and those only, who were from eternity chosen for salvation and given to him by the Father; that he should bestow upon them faith (which, together with all the other saving gifts of the Holy Spirit, he acquired for them by his death); that he should purify them by his blood from all sins, both original and actual, whether committed after or before believing; and having faithfully protected them even to the end, should finally establish them glorious before him, free from every spot and blemish.*

Here it seems that the Synod wants to nuance the classic sufficient-efficient distinction. Christ's death is sufficient for all but *intended* for the elect (note the emphasis on his will and intention, not just on efficacy). Allusions to Revelation 5, Ephesians 5, and several other texts show how steeped in scripture the delegates at Dort were and how they were attempting to frame their Articles in accordance with the Bible. The elect alone get the saving blessings and benefits of the cross, which include faith itself. What the Arminians saw as a condition for all, the Reformed here saw as a gift to the elect. As John Owen put it some years later, 'It is nowhere said in Scripture, nor can it reasonably be affirmed, that if we believe, Christ died for us (as though our believing should make that to be which otherwise was not,—the act create the object); but Christ died for us that we might believe. Salvation, indeed, is bestowed conditionally; but faith, which is the condition, is absolutely procured.'[102]

> 9. *This purpose, proceeding from eternal love towards the elect, has from the beginning of the world to this present time, been powerfully accomplished, and will henceforward still continue to be accomplished, the gates of hell opposing it in vain, so that the elect in their due times may be gathered together into one, and that there may always be a Church of believers, with its foundation in the blood of Christ, which may constantly love and perseveringly worship him as its Saviour (who, as a bridegroom for his bride, laid down his own life for her upon the cross), and which may celebrate him, both here and for all eternity.*

This does not deny that God has a love for all humanity in some sense. It affirms, nonetheless, that God's saving purpose and sending of Christ was 'for us and for our salvation.' The positive articles end with this lovely picture of the church celebrating Christ – both who he is and what he has done.

The Nicene Creed was very careful to say that Christ was 'begotten, not made.' The positive alone was not sufficient to counteract the error of those who made that Creed's careful stipulations necessary. In the same way, the Synod of Dort sought to address certain false accusations against their doctrines and reject various errors. These frame the positive articles so that they are less likely to be misunderstood or twisted in an opposing direction. Indeed, the 'rejection of errors' sections in the Canons of Dort 'best

---

[102] *Works*, 10: p 235.

expressed the primary intent of the Canons,' and in fact the 'positive sections expressing the orthodox Reformed view were added as an afterthought well into the synodical proceedings.'[103]

Rejection of Errors:

The true doctrine having been set out, the Synod rejects the errors of those:

1. *Who teach: That God the Father has ordained his Son to the death of the cross without a certain and definite purpose to save anyone in particular, so that the necessity, profitableness, and worth of what Christ obtained by his death might remain in good repair, perfect in all its parts, complete, and intact, even if the obtained redemption had never in fact been applied to any individual.*

   For this assertion is insulting to the wisdom of God the Father and the merits of Jesus Christ, and is contrary to Scripture. For thus says the Saviour: "I lay down my life for the sheep, and I know them" (John 10:15, 27). And concerning the Saviour, the prophet Isaiah says: "When you will make his soul a sacrifice for sin, he shall see his seed, he shall prolong his days, and the will of Jehovah shall prosper in his hand" (Isaiah 53:10). Finally, this overthrows the Article of Faith concerning the church of which we believe.

This opposes the idea of a random, indefinite atonement. The Canons also oppose those:

2. *Who teach: That it was not the goal of the death of Christ that he should confirm the new covenant of grace through his blood, but only that he should acquire for the Father the mere right to enter again with man any kind of covenant, whether of grace or of works.*

   For this is repugnant to Scripture which teaches that Christ hath become the surety and mediator of a better, that is, the

---

[103] D. Sinnema, 'The Canons of Dort: From Judgment on Arminianism to Confessional Standard,' in Goudriaan and Lieburg, *Revisiting the Synod of Dordt*, p 331.

new covenant (Hebrews 7:22), and "a testament is of force where there has been death" (Hebrews 9:15, 17).

This rejects the idea that the cross merely made it possible for God to start again with humanity. In the Trinitarian covenant doctrine of the Reformed at Dort, the Father gives the elect to the Son, who dies for them, and then gives them the Spirit and faith. As the seventeenth century progressed several Reformed theologians would further develop the doctrine of the intra-Trinitarian covenant of redemption, or *pactum salutis*, and utilise this harmonious agreement of the members of the Trinity in eternity to shape their understanding of the accomplishment and application of redemption.[104] Arminians could also employ the concept of an intra-Trinitarian pact,[105] but introduced their own distinctive views of human free will and conditionality further down the theological line in order to somewhat weaken its effectiveness. Several Remonstrant errors in covenant theology were rejected by the Synod, as unbiblical and tending towards Pelagianism or Socinianism. On the other hand, the Synod did not present or prescribe a fully worked out alternative federal structure, despite a covenantal flavour being apparent in many of the delegations' submissions. There was some diversity amongst the Reformed on this issue. They continued, however, to reject the teaching of those:

> 3. *Who teach: That Christ by his satisfaction did not certainly merit for anyone either salvation itself, or faith by which this satisfaction of Christ unto salvation may be effectually applied; but only that he acquired for the Father the power or the perfect will to deal anew with people, and to prescribe new conditions as he might will, the discharge of which should depend on the free will of man, so that it therefore might have come to pass that either none or all should fulfil them.*

---

[104] A good recent example of this can be seen in the clearly covenantal presentation of limited atonement in M.S. Horton, *The Christian Faith: A Systematic Theology for Pilgrims on the Way* (Grand Rapids: Zondervan, 2011), pp 516-520.

[105] On Arminius' use of the doctrine see R.A. Muller, 'Toward the Pactum Salutis: Locating the Origins of a Concept,' *Mid-America Journal of Theology* 18 (2007), pp 12-13 n14. The *Remonstrant Confession* 8:1 speaks of God proposing 'in himself' the work of redemption (*in se ipso proposuerat*). H. Hammond, *A Paraphrase & Annotations upon the Books of the Psalms* (London, 1683), p 8 refers to 'the covenant with and in Christ' in Psalm 2:7.

> *For these regard the death of Christ too dismissively, in no way acknowledge the most important fruit or benefit gained by it, and bring again out of hell the error of the Pelagians.*

Note again the mention of faith itself being a gift from God, purchased by the atonement – one of the most important benefits and fruits of the cross. This paragraph rejects the idea of salvation being contingent on our use of our 'free will,' and ascribes each part of it to God. Arminius considered the cross to have removed obstacles from God's way so that he was now able to forgive if people had faith. God was inclined to forgive before, but justice prevented him. For Arminius, the cross did not actually achieve forgiveness, redemption, or justification.[106] Arminian errors were considered by many to be perilously close to the ancient heresy of Pelagius, which Augustine had fought against with the doctrines of grace and was condemned by the early church. Some later Arminians were bold enough to identify themselves openly with Pelagius.[107]

> 4. *Who teach: That this new covenant of grace, which God the Father made with people, through the intervention of the death of Christ, does not consist in this: that we by faith, in as much as it lays hold on the merits of Christ, are justified before God and saved; but that God, having revoked the demand for perfect obedience to the law, regards faith itself and the imperfect obedience of faith, as perfect obedience to the law, and graciously assesses it worthy of the reward of eternal life through grace.*

> *For these contradict Scripture: "Being justified freely by his grace through the redemption that is in Christ Jesus, whom God set forth to be a propitiation, through faith in his blood" (Romans 3:23-24). And these introduce, as did the wicked Socinus, a new and strange justification of man before God, against the consensus of the whole Church.*

---

[106] *The Writings of James Arminius*, 3: pp 352-353.

[107] For example, John Wesley was happy to identify with Pelagius who he saw as a true Christian, a holy man, and part of the righteous remnant in church history, unfairly stigmatized as a heretic by an angry and abusive Augustine who was not worth listening to. See *The Works of John Wesley* (Grand Rapids: Baker, 2007), 6: pp 328-329.

This again rejects an erroneous Arminian view of the new covenant of grace, which imagines that God accepts our faith (freely-willed, so to speak) and our subsequent imperfect works as good enough for heaven. So, the teaching goes, God used to demand that we obey his law perfectly to be saved; now he simply wants us to trust him, do what we can, however imperfectly, and that will be enough to earn heaven. This was equated with the teaching of Socinus, an anti-Trinitarian and arch-heretic as far as the Reformed of the seventeenth century were concerned. Many Arminians had close links with the Socinians at this time, and some had even infamously crossed the line and joined them. Arminians were not of necessity anti-Trinitarian, but did share other presuppositions with this group, including very similar approaches to biblical interpretation. It might be said that, notwithstanding their differences, both Arminians and Socinians were the vanguards of theological liberalism in their day.

> 5. *Who teach: That all people have been accepted into the state of reconciliation and the grace of the covenant, so that no one is liable to damnation or must be damned because of original sin, but that all are exempt from the guilt of that sin.*
>
> *For this judgment is repugnant to the Scripture which affirms that "we are by nature children of wrath" (Ephesians 2:3).*

Arminians taught that original sin had been wiped out by the coming of Christ, so that anyone could now freely choose to accept Christ if they wanted to. This was opposed to the Reformed view of original sin and the bondage of the will, taught effectively in the previous century by Luther against the Dutch humanist Erasmus, who in many ways was a forerunner of the Remonstrants.

> 6. *Who seize upon the distinction between obtaining and applying, to the end that they may instil into the minds of the unwary and inexperienced this teaching, that God, as far as he is concerned, has willed to apply to all people equally the benefits acquired by the death of Christ; but that, while some are made partakers of the forgiveness of sins and eternal life, and others are not, this difference depends on their own free will, which applies itself to the grace that is offered indifferently, and that it is not dependent on the special gift of mercy, effectually working in them, that they rather than others should apply this grace to themselves.*

For these, while they pretend that they propose this distinction in a sound sense, seek to make people drink the pernicious poison of Pelagianism.

Arminianism is again likened in some respects to the Pelagian heresy. Once more, the main point at issue was free will and faith, and whether everything hinges on our personal acceptance of Christ or whether he has done everything necessary to save us completely. They are attacked here for misuse of scholastic distinctions. The consensus amongst Reformed theologians was to see the obtaining and applying of redemption as being coterminous, that is, those for whom Christ obtained redemption (in his death) certainly received its benefits.

> 7. *Who teach: That neither Christ could die, nor needed to die, and also did not die, for those whom God most highly loved and chose for eternal life, since these do not need the death of Christ.*
>
> *For they contradict the apostle, who says: "Christ loved me and gave himself up for me" (Galatians 2:20). Likewise, "Who shall lay anything to the charge of God's elect? It is God that justifies; who is he that condemns? It is Christ Jesus that died..." (Romans 8:33-34), namely, for them; and the Saviour who asserts: "I lay down my life for the sheep" (John 10:15). And, "This is my commandment that you love one another, even as I have loved you. Greater love has no one than this, that someone should lay down his life for his friends" (John 15:12-13).*

This sounds to us like a very strange thing to have to deny, that the elect did not need Christ to die for them. It was, however, a common misunderstanding, and something Arminians attempted to press against the Reformed. For example, in their post-Dort, 1621 Confession they suggest that surely 'those who are predestinated unto Life, have no need of any such Expiation' because they are already 'beloved of God with the highest love.'[108] To guard against this

---

[108] See Simon Episcopius, *The Confession or Declaration of the... Remonstrants* (London, 1676), pp 136-37 (Article 8.10).

calumny, the Reformed decided to explicitly reject it as an unwarranted logical inference from their doctrine.

The Canons of Dort are a classic statement of Reformed doctrine of the atonement: anti-Arminian on the one hand, and yet moderate when compared with some of the more rigidly particularistic predestinarian theologies around at the time. It is vital to note what the points at issue were at Dort, what was said and what was not said. The Lombardian formula of 'sufficient for all, efficacious for the elect' is not employed in quite the way it had been previously. While many could see the usefulness of such a memorable distinction it was not universally popular with Calvinists. Calvin himself, though he admitted the truth of it, thought it irrelevant where others often invoked it,[109] and while many delegations did utilise a form of it in their submissions, the Genevans at Dort refused to.[110]

No-one wanted to deny the infinite worth and sufficiency of the atonement – see positive Articles 3 and 6 above – but they wanted to avoid the impression that it was ever God's plan to actually save everyone through this infinitely sufficient sacrifice. Blacketer and Cunningham both highlight that the sufficient-efficient formula can be misused or misinterpreted in such a way that an Arminian could affirm it, which would of course make it less useful in this polemical context, and that it lacks the key element of clearly defining God's intention.[111] Indeed, Arminius himself approved of the sufficient-efficient formula,[112] which shows that it is not entirely adequate to simply regurgitate what Lombard said, as if that settles the question as it has been posed since the seventeenth century.[113] The element of 'intent' in the atonement also needs to be defined.

---

[109] E.g. *Calvin's Commentaries Volume XXII*, 173 (on 1 John 2:2). That is not to say he *rejected* it, as Kendall suggests. Cf. Helm, *Calvin and the Calvinists*, p 39.

[110] As did the delegations from Emden, Overijsel, and North Holland. See Thomas, *Extent*, pp 138-140.

[111] Blacketer, 'Definite Atonement', p 311. Cunningham, *Historical Theology*, 2: p 332.

[112] *Writings*, 3: p 345.

[113] As Andrew D. Naselli says in 'John Owen's Argument for Definite Atonement in *The Death of Death in the Death of Christ*: A Summary and Evaluation,' in *The Southern Baptist Journal of Theology* 14.4 (Winter 2010), p 74, 'Although the phrase may defuse tensions in many situations, it blurs distinctions and, therefore, is unhelpful to use for defining a position.'

At Dort, advocates of this doctrine explicitly framed their doctrine so as to rule out potentially erroneous conclusions (e.g. certain hyper-calvinist errors) in the same way those in the patristic period guarded the doctrine of the Trinity from the errors of tritheism or modalism. So that to accuse limited atonement of implying a lack of evangelism or say that it leads to a narrow-minded, insular faith would be on a par with accusing Athanasius of being a 'potential' tri-theist – it ignores what was specifically affirmed and denied. Moreover, of course, later advocates of Dort's doctrine such as George Whitefield and Charles Spurgeon are among the most successful evangelists in history and rejected hyper-Calvinism in their example as well as their teaching.[114]

3.4. Hypothetical Universalism and the Impact of Dort

The British delegation at Dort were divided about the atonement. Most were happy with the majority view, but John Davenant and Samuel Ward sought a middle way. They won the day as far as the British submission to the Synod went. This suggested that Christ 'died for all, that all and every one by means of faith might obtain remission of sins, and eternal life by virtue of that ransom. But Christ so died for the elect, that by the merit of his death in special manner... they might infallibly obtain both faith and eternal life.'[115] So as well as dying efficaciously for the elect, Christ also intended to die conditionally for all, so that hypothetically all were savable. This is the doctrine which came to be known as hypothetical universalism. John Cameron, an early advocate of this position, unwraps the basic idea in a famous illustration of how the cross works differently for the elect and unelect: the sun shines equally upon all men, but some sleep, while others open their eyes.[116] If they opened their eyes they would see light, but they do not.

Perhaps the 'strictest' Calvinists at the Synod were the Genevan delegation. Although they disagreed with this hypothetical

---

[114] See, especially, I. Murray, *Spurgeon and Hyper-Calvinism: The Battle for Gospel Preaching* (Edinburgh: Banner of Truth, 1995).

[115] See the Latin in *Acta* 2: p 79.

[116] See S. Strehle, 'Universal Grace and Amyraldianism,' in *Westminster Theological Journal* 51.2 (Fall 1989), p 347 n11.

universalist view, they did not, however, see it as a grave threat to the church, as they did Arminianism.[117] Many have speculated about the impact which British insistence on these points may have had on the text of the Canons. Article 2.8, for example, affirms that God 'willed that Christ ...should *effectually* (*efficaciter*) redeem ...all those, and those only, who were from eternity chosen.' As Jonathan Moore points out, this left a backdoor open for Davenant and others by not technically denying an ultimately *ineffectual* universal redemption in addition to this.[118] Neither do the Canons definitively rule out a 'complex-intention' view that might posit multiple divine intentions (i.e. Christ came to save the elect *and* to make others 'saveable'). Other Reformed statements on the subject *were* phrased in such a way as to exclude this view, but Dort refrained from doing so.[119] It is clear then that the Calvinism of Dort is neither monolithic nor uncompromising, and that it was 'the expression of a laborious theological compromise worked out between the various Calvinist traditions.'[120]

It is vitally important to note that the hypothetically universalist view had something of a heritage in Britain, being privately held by no less a man than the influential Irish Archbishop, James Ussher. In a letter dated March 3rd 1617, unpublished until after his death but widely copied, circulated, and talked about, he made the following distinction: 'The *satisfaction* of Christ, onely makes the sinnes of mankind *fit for pardon*... The particular *application* makes the sins of those to whom that mercy is vouchsafed to be *actually pardoned*... [B]y the vertue of this blessed Oblation, God is made *placable* unto our *nature*... but not *actually* appeased with

---

[117] N. Fornerod, 'A Reappraisal of the Genevan Delegation at the Synod of Dordt,' in Goudriaan and Lieburg, *Revisiting the Synod of Dordt*, pp 211-212.

[118] Jonathan Moore, 'The Extent of the Atonement,' in Michael Haykin and Mark Jones (eds.), *Drawn into Controversie: Reformed Theological Diversity and Debates within Seventeenth-Century British Puritanism* (Göttingen: Vandenhoeck & Ruprecht, 2011), pp 145–146.

[119] *Synopsis Purioris Theologiae* (Leiden, 1625), XXIX.xxix says, for example, that 'the end, object, and "for whom" ($\tilde{\omega}$ or *cui*) of satisfaction is only Elect and true believers,' which *would* I think exclude the British hypothetical universalist view.

[120] Fornerod, 'A Reappraisal,' p 183; Robert Godfrey, 'Tensions within International Calvinism: The Debate on the Atonement at the Synod of Dort' (Ph.D., Stanford University, 1974), p 268.

any, until he hath received his Son.'[121] He added that 'the universality of the satisfaction derogates nothing from the necessity of the speciall Grace in the application'[122] and that 'in one respect [Christ] may be said to have *died for all*, and in another respect *not* to have died for all.'[123]

Nearly thirty years after Dort, in October 1646 the Westminster Assembly of Divines also debated the issue of the extent of the atonement.[124] Scene One of the debate revolved around whether it is possible to dissent from particular redemption without being an Arminian. In the opening exchanges it was the Arminian question which was at the forefront of the delegates' minds and Edmund Calamy opened by attempting to distance himself from the Remonstrants. 'I am farre from universall Redemption in the Arminian sence,' he began, 'but that that I hould is in the sence of our devines in the sinod of Dort.'[125] He fleshes this out by asserting that Christ 'did pay a price for all, absolute <intention> for the elect, conditionall <intention> for the reprobate, in case they doe believe.'[126]

There are various parallels between the positions of Ussher, Davenant, and Calamy. Indeed, Jonathan Moore shows that Ussher had been exerting influence behind the scenes for many years, trying to win the next generation of theologians to his 'middle way' position. He would speak about it to people but did not go into print to express his concerns in a way that could be openly debated or examined in his lifetime. Yet his opinion circulated in manuscript form amongst those in the circle, and as they built a bridgehead into the church they spread their mediating influence.[127] It had its effect not only at Dort but also at Westminster.

---

[121] J. Ussher, *The Judgement of the late Archbishop of Armagh and Primate of Ireland, 1. Of the extent of Christs death and satisfaction* (London, 1658), pp 4-5.
[122] *Ibid.*, p 13.
[123] *Ibid.*, p 15.
[124] For more on the details concerning the Westminster Assembly debate see Lee Gatiss, '"Shades of Opinion within a Generic Calvinism": The Particular Redemption Debate at the Westminster Assembly,' in *Reformed Theological Review* 69.2 (2010).
[125] Van Dixhoorn, 'Reforming the Reformation', 6: p 202.
[126] *Ibid.*, p 203. The words in parentheses are interlined in the text of the Minutes.
[127] Moore, *English Hypothetical Universalism*, p 212.

Although there were complaints that French Reformed theologian Moses Amyraut was behind this 'middle way' as presented at the Assembly, Calamy and his position is not best labelled Amyraldian. It is true that Amyraut did quickly become *the* name attached to the Reformed variant of 'universal redemption.' Yet to call all exponents of 'middle way' positions 'Amyraldian' is not entirely accurate. Amyraut's position depended on some other distinctive doctrines which were not and are not shared by all 'hypothetical universalists.' For example, his speculative ordering of the moments in God's decree as well as his view on original sin and moral and natural ability found him on trial at Alençon in 1637.[128] He also held a unique and distinctive view on the Trinity which flowed from his understanding of redemption, but which was not shared by other 'universal redemptionists.'[129]

Amyraut's doctrine of hypothetical universalism is most clearly presented in his *Brief Traitté de la Predestination* (1634). This was intended to present the doctrine of predestination 'in a manner which would give the least offense to Catholics,' and find common ground with them, especially the Catholic nobility with whom he was friendly, but also to Lutherans.[130] In the *Brief Tract*, he speaks of Christ coming 'to procure the salvation of the human race.'[131] Since, he says, the misery of men is universal, and God's desire to deliver proceeds from his compassion for all the fallen, who are equally his creatures, 'the grace of redemption which [Christ] has offered and procured for them had to be universal.'[132] He adds that this is 'provided that they also are all disposed to receive it.' So there is a condition, but Christ's propitiatory sacrifice was offered for all and

---

[128] Armstrong, *Calvinism and the Amyraut Heresy*, pp 88-96.

[129] *Ibid.*, pp 172-177.

[130] Lum, *Brief Treatise on Predestination*, pp i, ix, xi. Amyraut was a member of the aristocracy himself and was keen to pursue ecumenical relations with the Lutherans. It is worth noting that Amyraut's approach, while within the bounds of Reformed thought, seems to share with Rome and the Remonstrants a 'possibility-realization scheme.'

[131] 'Procurer le salut du genre humain.' Amyraut, *Brief Traitté* (1658), p 62.

[132] 'La grace de la redemption qu'il leur a offerte & procurée a deu estre universelle.' Amyraut, *Brief Traite*, p 65.

intended for all.[133] No nation or individual is excluded by the will of God from the salvation he has acquired for the human race, provided that they make use of the testimonies to God's mercy given to them.[134] Theoretically, some may be saved without knowing the name of Christ; they believe in him 'without knowing who is the author of the mercy.'[135] God's wrath is appeased and the barrier of sin removed so that anyone can be forgiven *if* they are not unworthy (*indignes*).[136]

Amyraut cites 1 Timothy 2:4 'God desires the salvation of all.' Yet he adds that there must be a gloss, a limitation put on this verse. God desires all to be saved but only 'provided that they believe... if they do not believe, he does not desire it.'[137] The nature of man being what it is, the cross would have been entirely useless and had no effect unless God stepped in to also make some believe and embrace the grace offered to us.[138] Christ was therefore abandoned to the death of the cross 'for the universal salvation of the world' but God does not wish this to be of any use to us unless we believe and therefore repent.[139] The grace which grants repentance is not universal; indeed, only a very small number are elect says Amyraut. If people do not

---

[133] *Ibid.*, p 66: 'a esté pour tous... est destiné à tous.' In 1634, the text read 'est destiné *egalement* pour tous' ('*equally* for all,' or '*in the same way* for all', my emphasis) but this was amended in the new corrected and revised edition of 1658. In the same way, the 1634 edition made both misery and grace '*equal* and universal,' but in 1658 this becomes simply 'universal.'

[134] *Ibid.*, p 68: 'il ne faut pas penser pourtant qu'il y ait ny aucun peuple, ny mesmes aucun homme exclus par la volonté de Dieu, du salut qu'il a acquis au genre humain.'

[135] *Ibid.*, pp 69-72: 'persuadés sans le connoistre de la misericoree dont il est auteur.' Amyraut later denied that anyone is saved this way.

[136] This is *similar* to, but less optimistic than, Roman Catholic dogma, which affirms that, 'the plan of salvation also includes those who acknowledge the Creator. In the first place amongst these there are the Mohammedans, who, professing to hold the faith of Abraham, along with us adore the one and merciful God, who on the last day will judge mankind. Nor is God far distant from those who in shadows and images seek the unknown God, for it is He who gives to all men life and breath and all things, and as Saviour wills that all men be saved (1 Timothy 2:4).' *Dogmatic Constitution of the Church: Lumen Gentium* (1964), chapter 2, number 16.

[137] Amyraut, *Brief Traitté*, p 76: 'S'ils ne croyent point , il ne le veut pas.'

[138] *Ibid.*, p 88: '...pour le faire croire & embrasser la grace qui luy est offerte.'

[139] *Ibid.*, p 89: 'pour le salut du monde universel... foy au Redempteur, laquelle se tesmoigne en repentance. Sans cela il ne veut pas que cette sienne misericorde nous soit d'aucun usage.'

believe, it is not God's fault but theirs (their unbelief does not come from their reprobation).[140]

Amyraut also distinguishes between what he calls 'predestination to salvation' and 'predestination to faith.'[141] Predestination to salvation is universal and conditional; but predestination to faith is particular and unconditional. Those who do not believe frustrate the first predestination and the purpose of Christ's death. This is Amyraut's explanation for why there are both universal and particular statements about the cross in scripture, though he confesses that scripture, and especially Paul, speaks of Christ's coming as if it had been ordained only for the elect and not for others.[142] By expounding two predestinations this way he believes he can avoid the accusation (the 'horrible confusion!') that the predestined are saved regardless of what they do, and the reprobate damned regardless of what they do – an old but crude suggestion.[143]

John Davenant, however, learned his hypothetical universalism well before Amyraut had even begun to study theology. He was better known amongst English divines in the first half of the seventeenth century. Their position is not *mere* 'hypothetical universalism,' which is, as Alan Clifford rightly says, 'a description more applicable to the Arminians,'[144] since they also believed in an absolute redemption of the elect (which the Arminians did not). More accurately, therefore, Davenant, Calamy, and others like them might be called Calvinistic hypothetical universalists of a British variety (as opposed to the French version of Amyraut, with its own peculiar twists).[145]

This middle position has been criticised on various fronts, but one of the most pertinent is that it seems to be pointless. As Roger

---

[140] *Ibid.*, pp 92-93.

[141] *Ibid.*, p 138. On his later 'clarification', see *Synodicon in Gallia Reformata* (London, 1692), 2: p 355.

[142] *Ibid.*, p 164. Cf. p 82.

[143] *Ibid.*, pp 140-142. This ridiculous idea was used in an attempt to discredit the doctrine of predestination in the ninth century by Rabanus Maurus, and in the eighteenth century by John Wesley. See *Patrologia Latina* 112:155c and L. Gatiss, *The True Profession of the Gospel: Augustus Toplady and Reclaiming our Reformed Foundations* (London: Latimer Trust, 2010), pp 95-96.

[144] A.C. Clifford, *Atonement and Justification: English Evangelical Theology 1640-1790* (Oxford: Clarendon, 1990), p 154.

[145] I am not sure they would rejoice in the acronym CHUB!

Nicole puts it: 'On the hypothetical-universalists' own showing, since no one has faith but those to whom it is efficaciously given by God, a universal redemption on condition of faith is not a blessing which issues in any concrete advantage to the non-elect. In this light the vaunted benevolence of God toward all mankind appears as nugatory.'[146] In other words, why create the entirely empty set of 'people who would be saved by the universal atonement *if* they believed, but who won't believe because God will not grant them faith'?

A century after the Westminster Assembly, Isaac Watts expressed a ˙similar hypothetical universalist position. 'It seems evident to me from several texts of the word of God,' he wrote, 'that Christ did not die with an equal design for all men; but that there is a special number whom the Father chose and gave to the Son, whose salvation is absolutely secured by the death and intercession of Christ; John xvii. 6, 9, 10.' So far so Calvinistic. 'But why,' Watts continues, 'should this hinder our interpretation of some other texts in a more general and catholic sense... Why may we not suppose conditional pardon and conditional salvation... to be the purchase of the death of Christ?'[147] The answer from Dort and Westminster would be, 'Why *should* we suppose such contingency in God?' Was there any good reason in scripture to assign a conditional element to the eternal plan of God, that God would somehow not be certain of and which in actual fact would not result in anyone but the elect taking up the offer? As Robert Harris put it on the floor of the Westminster Assembly, 'I doubt whether ther be any such thing at all as conditionall decree.'[148] He was puzzled by the idea of a condition being set in God's decree which the reprobate could not perform anyway and 'God never intends to give them[!].'[149]

The text of the Westminster Confession on God's eternal decree (WCF 3.6) ended up being not quite as particularistic as it might have been, as a result of Calamy's influence. It does not say 'no-one is redeemed by Christ but the elect only.' In the context of the

[146] R. Nicole, 'The Case for Definite Atonement' in *Bulletin of the Evangelical Theological Society* 10.4 (1967), p 203. 'Nugatory' means trifling, worthless, futile.
[147] I. Watts, *The Ruin and Recovery of Mankind* (London, 1742), p 263.
[148] Van Dixhoorn, 'Reforming the Reformation', 6: p 211.
[149] Van Dixhoorn, 'Reforming the Reformation', 6: p 203.

debate, this statement would have emphatically limited the atonement to the elect only and clearly excluded Calamy's view. The final text of the Confession reads, 'Neither are any other redeemed by Christ, effectually called, justified, adopted, sanctified, and saved, but the elect only.'[150] This carefully limits to the elect not the atonement / redemption *per se*, but the whole of salvation, obtained *and* applied.[151] A hypothetical universalist of Calamy's sophistication would not have disputed this.

That being said, it seems a majority in the Assembly disagreed with Calamy. In his reply, Edward Reynolds said of Calamy's view that it 'cannot be asserted by any that can say he is not of the Remonstrants opinion.'[152] In other words, he accused Calamy of only a pretended distance between himself and the Arminians, averring at the very least that the middle way is a slippery slope. The more consistently particularist position was not defended in a uniform theological manner by the other Westminster Divines, or with homogenous exegetical tactics; they disagreed among themselves over the precise way to interpret John 3:16 for example, and on the proper theological grounding for the universal offer of the gospel (as the Reformed had also done at Dort). However, they were able to agree that 'To all those for whom Christ hath purchased Redemption, he doth certainly, and effectually apply, and communicate the same.'[153]

They also agreed in chapter 7 section 3 of the *Westminster Confession* that the gospel should be freely offered to sinners, with faith being required for salvation but with a promise to the elect that

---

[150] See *The Humble Advice of the Assembly of Divines... Concerning a Confession of Faith* (London, 1647), pp 7-8. I have also had the privilege of examining the original handwritten autograph held at Westminster College, Cambridge to check that there are commas between items here as opposed to slashes or the word 'or' which may change the interpretation.

[151] I am of course aware that this understanding is disputed by some fine interpreters of the Confession such as A.A. Hodge, but I believe they are guilty of special pleading here, and strain the grammar of WCF 3.6. For in-depth argument on the nuances of the Confession in the light of the contemporary debates, see Lee Gatiss, 'A Deceptive Clarity? Particular Redemption in the Westminster Standards,' in *Reformed Theological Review* 69.3 (2010).

[152] Van Dixhoorn, 'Reforming the Reformation', 6: p 203.

[153] *Westminster Confession of Faith* 8.8.

the Spirit would give such to them. This is not, as some have thought, a 'compromise between conditional universalism taught in the first clause, and particular election taught in the second.'[154] Rather it is an affirmation of both particular election and universal offer in their proper places and relations. Chapter 3 on God's eternal decree was the place to confess truths about election and divine intentionality; Chapter 7 on the covenant was the place to confess the complimentary truth of the gospel offer, and to mention the promise of the Spirit who applies election through faith. One has reference to God's eternal perspective, the other to his temporal dealings with humanity.

Richard Baxter claimed that he had been told by an eminent member of the Assembly that they had purposely avoided a decisive determination of this controversy between shades of opinion within a generic Calvinism.[155] As at Dort, they wanted to oppose Arminianism but keep the Calvinist coalition together. Whether that is true or not, at Westminster and Dort the 'Davenant men' failed to get their opinions distinctly sanctioned, though they did, it seems, force the two august gatherings to express themselves very carefully and in such a way that they could assent to.

According to Richard Muller, one of world's foremost experts in seventeenth century theology, the views of Amyraldians and other Calvinistic hypothetical universalists during this formative period of Reformed theology, 'were not heresy and, like it or not, were consciously framed to stand within the confessionalism of the Canons of Dort.'[156] Although some accused Amyraut of being an Arminian, and of unsettling people with new vocabulary and new distinctions, he did in fact teach standard Reformed doctrines such as total depravity, irresistible grace, perseverance of the saints, and

---

[154] See Schaff, *The Creeds of Christendom*, 1: pp 772-773, who erroneously thinks this 'is in substance the theory of the school of Saumur' (i.e. Amyraldianism).

[155] See the Preface to Baxter, *Certain Disputations of Right to Sacraments, and the True Nature of Visible Christianity* (London, 1657).

[156] R.A. Muller, 'Divine Covenants, Absolute and Conditional: John Cameron and the Early Orthodox Development of Reformed Covenant Theology' in *Mid-America Journal of Theology* 17 (2006), p 36.

infralapsarianism.[157] What he and other Calvinistic hypothetical universalists held to were in fact variants of limited atonement, because they did see a definite, limited intent in the atonement towards the elect. They added a conditional intent on top of this or prior to this (not *instead of* this, as Arminians do).

This is distinctive and must be justified scripturally somehow (especially if it begins speculatively to tamper with the order of God's decrees).[158] But the generally Calvinistic substructure of the position ought to be acknowledged, defended (by its advocates), and spoken of more often than it usually is. Otherwise, Reformed communities in which the only thing young theologians pick up is that being classically Reformed on this issue is for some reason disapproved of, could easily degenerate into Arminianism within a generation.

3.5. *The Anglican view*

Roman Catholicism tends more to the Arminian way of seeing these things, as we have already noted. In the seventeenth century, however, there was one exception. A Catholic group called the Jansenists (which included, most famously, Blaise Pascal) had a much more Augustinian view of soteriology in general. The Jesuits opposed them, and set down their doctrine in five specific points. According to one of these, the

---

[157] See S. Strehle, 'Universal Grace and Amyraldianism' in *Westminster Theological Journal* 51.2 (Fall 1989), pp 349-350. Strehle adds 'double predestination' to this list. Amyraut says in *Brief Traitté*, p 146 that although God predestines some to believe, 'il n'a pas predestiné les autres à ne croire pas' (he has not predestined the others not to believe). So it is perhaps better to say that he holds to predestination and preterition (not predamnation). See above for Amyraut's views on the two kinds of predestination (to salvation, and to faith), which is a different kind of 'double' predestination.

[158] John Davenant's *Dissertatio de Morte Christi* (1650), p 88 discusses the order of decrees as a 'thorny little question [*spinosam quaestiunculam*] which has been thrown around by many [*à multis vexatam*], and is throwing [*vexantem*] all who have taken it up.' Even if, he says, one conceives of the decree to send Christ as Mediator as if it preceded the decree to infallibly choose certain people for eternal life, it cannot be torn apart from the fact that from eternity Christ is foreseen as dying in a special way for those chosen. He then looks at it the other way around, but in the end this whole discussion is dismissed as 'a triflingly unnecessary thing.' He then proposes his own thesis concerning 'the death of Christ as limited (*restrictâ*) by some special consideration to those predestined alone.' Others are not so restrained and careful in their discussion of this issue.

Jansenists believed that, 'It is Semipelagian to say that Christ died and shed his blood for all men.'[159] They were close, it seems, to the Reformed view of the extent of the atonement.

This view, however, was officially condemned by Pope Innocent X in 1653. So the official Roman position appears to be that it is not Semipelagian to say Christ died for all. Indeed, the Pope went on to say that this saying extracted from Jansen's book on Augustine was 'Declared and condemned as false, rash, scandalous, and understood in this sense, "that Christ died for the salvation of the predestined," impious, blasphemous, contumelious, dishonoring to divine piety, and heretical.'[160]

Amongst Anglicans, there has sometimes been debate over what the official position of the Church of England is on this issue. Do the official formularies of the Church of England have anything to say on the subject which would bind confessional Anglicans to a particular view? Some have claimed that Article 31 of *The Thirty-nine Articles of Religion* settles the issue against limited atonement: 'The Offering of Christ once made is that perfect redemption, propitiation, and satisfaction for all the sins of the whole world, both original and actual.'[161]

This is the line taken by Terry Miethe in *The Grace of God, The Will of Man: A Case for Arminianism*. In a personal attack, he questions how Jim Packer can be both an advocate of limited atonement and an Anglican minister.[162] Miethe also claims, along with the respected Anglican theologian David Broughton Knox, that

---

[159] 'Jansenism: The "Five Propositions", 1653,' in Henry Bettenson and Chris Maunder (eds.), *Documents of the Christian Church: 4th Edition* (Oxford: Oxford University Press, 2011), p 273.

[160] Heinrich Denzinger, *The Sources of Catholic Dogma* (London: Herder Book Company, 1957), p 316. Cf. *Catechism of the Catholic Church*, #605.

[161] See for instance how Article 31 (and the BCP Catechism) were used by John McLeod Campbell in his heresy trial in Tuttle, *So Rich an Soil*, p 47. Cf. Lightner, *The Death Christ Died*, p 13.

[162] See T.L. Miethe, 'The Universal Power of the Atonement', p 88. He also cites similar words from the Holy Communion service in the *Book of Common Prayer* in support of this contention. Packer, of course, famously wrote the preface to a reprint of John Owen's *Death of Death in the Death of Christ*, which is reprinted in his *Among God's Giants* (Eastbourne: Kingsway, 1991), pp 163-195 and is a clear and classic statement of the gospel with limited atonement at its heart.

the *BCP*'s Catechism teaches unlimited atonement when it asks 'What dost thou chiefly learn in these Articles of thy Belief?' and the answer is given, 'I learn to believe in... God the Son, Who hath redeemed me, and all mankind.'[163]

The use of the Catechism and Prayer Book to oppose limited atonement goes back at least to Francis White at the York House Conference in 1626. He used those documents to pillory some aspects of the Synod of Dort's teaching as inconsistent with the Church of England's doctrine. For example, he said, 'The Dortists... have denied that Christ died for all men.' On such a basis 'how could we say to all communicants whatsoever "The Body of our Lord which was given for thee," as we are bound to say?'[164]

Apart from the fact that the British delegates at Dort were very careful not to allow anything that contradicted 'the confession of the Church of England' into the Canons of Dort,[165] this statement about the Communion service fails to take account of the liturgical setting of those words. Those to whom the bread and wine are offered should just previously have confessed their 'manifold sins and wickedness' and thrown themselves on God's mercy in Christ using the prayer of confession. They will also have declared their faith in the words of the creed: the Nicene Creed declares that 'for us and for our salvation he came down from heaven' just as the Athanasian Creed affirms that he 'suffered for us' – that is, those who say 'We believe...' So none of these liturgical texts express a universal atonement: they express limited atonement in a covenantal context where believers are charitably presumed to be the elect for whom Christ died, just as in various biblical texts: 1 Corinthians 11:24; Romans 5:8; Galatians 1:3-4; 1 Thessalonians 5:9-10; 1 Peter 2:24; and Titus 2:14.

Other texts in the formularies have occasionally been cited (less successfully) in this debate, including the General Thanksgiving prayer which thanks God for 'for thine inestimable love in the redemption of the world by our Lord Jesus Christ.' Augustus Toplady argued with Dr. Nowell that 'thou didst open the kingdom of heaven to all believers' in

---

[163] See Miethe, *ibid.*, p 95 n45, and Knox, 'Some Aspects', p 262.
[164] N. Tyacke, *Anti-Calvinists: The Rise of English Arminianism c.1590-1640* (Oxford: Clarendon Press, 1987), pp 176-177.
[165] See Moore, 'James Ussher's Influence,' p 175.

the *Te Deum* cannot be used to prove Arminianism in the Prayer Book.[166] Often in such instances, neither side is particularly convincing! The Catechism text used by Miethe is ambiguous at best, yet if it *could* be shown to be an assertion of unlimited atonement it would also have to be admitted that as a summary of the second article of the Apostles Creed (which is what it is supposed to be) it says rather more than is warranted by that Creed itself.

One of the prayers for the Ember Weeks, for those who are about to be ordained, begins 'Almighty God, our heavenly Father, who hast purchased to thyself an universal church by the precious blood of thy dear Son...' This sounds fairly 'definite' regarding the atonement, which actually purchased a specific group, the church. It ends, however, speaking about the function of the ordained being to 'set forward the salvation of all men', which could sound like universal atonement (or even universal salvation!). So care must be taken when handling these texts doctrinally.[167]

Other prayers which may speak to this issue include the first Collect for Good Friday in which it is said that Christ suffered death for 'this thy family,' and also the Collect for the second Sunday after Easter which addresses God, 'who hast given thine only Son to be unto *us*... a sacrifice for sin.' In my view it is most natural to read these as referring to 'us, this assembled congregation of believers praying the Collect.' So they are in no way contrary to limited atonement even if they are not quite water-tight proof of its appearance in the Prayer Book.

Jim Packer's withering response to his assailant regarding Article 31 is that 'Miethe's whole discussion is unsatisfying... he treats echoes of biblical phraseology in sixteenth-century Anglican formularies as the Church of England taking sides in a seventeenth-century debate'.[168] He is referring to the Article's echoing of 1 John 2:2 that the cross was for the 'sins of the whole world'. Interestingly neither the Article nor the Communion liturgy quote that verse's

---

[166] Toplady, *Complete Works*, p 641.
[167] My own reading of this is that it refers more to a universal offer of salvation to all rather than a universal atonement or universal salvation. Alluding to 1 Timothy 4:16, the prayer teaches that we are to show all people (our hearers), through our lives and doctrine, how they can be saved.
[168] Packer, 'The Love of God,' p 289.

negative assertion that Christ was a propitiation for our sins '*and not for ours only*', which may have made this a more persuasive argument for the Arminian case. It is also certainly suggestive that none of the standard commentaries on the Articles, even Arminian ones, make any comment on the extent of the atonement under Article 31.[169] It is simply not what this Article is concerned with. That being said, Arminian misuse of Article 31 did lead the Westminster Assembly to sharpen up the parallel statement in the *Westminster Confession* 29.2. They say that the cross is 'the alone propitiation for all the sins of his elect.' The *Thirty-nine Articles* are not a broadening Arminian response to this 'narrow' focus, but an earlier allusion to biblical language which was afterwards misappropriated by a theology alien to the tenor of the Articles as a whole. Whether the Westminster divines were right in their own confession to subtly amend the language or not, their motives in doing so are perhaps apparent, and entirely understandable.

Apart from Packer's accusation of anachronism (which may not be precisely accurate considering what was said above about pre-seventeenth century awareness of the question) there is even more that could be said against Arminian exegesis of the Anglican formularies. Considered in the context of the rest of Article 31 itself, it is clear that the disputed line in the first half of the Article is intimately linked to the assertion in the second part against the Roman Catholic Mass. To quote the Article in full:

Of the one oblation of Christ finished upon the cross

The Offering of Christ once made is that perfect redemption, propitiation, and satisfaction, for all the sins of the whole world, both original and actual; and there is none other satisfaction for sin, but that alone. Wherefore the sacrifices of Masses, in which it was commonly said, that the Priest did offer Christ for the quick

---

[169] See my *The True Profession of the Gospel*, pp 90-91 where I cite evidence for this from about a dozen commentaries, to which we may now also add M. Jensen and T. Frame, *Defining Convictions and Decisive Commitments: The Thirty-nine Articles in Contemporary Anglicanism* (Canberra: Barton Books, 2010) which again stresses the sufficiency of the atonement here. G. Bray, *The Faith We Confess: An Exposition of the Thirty-nine Articles* (London: Latimer Trust, 2009) does make some very helpful comments on the debate in his exposition of Article 31, taking a clearly Reformed line.

and the dead, to have remission of pain or guilt, were blasphemous fables, and dangerous deceits.

Thus it is abundantly plain that this Article, when read in its immediate context, is an assertion of the *sufficiency* of the atonement designed to undercut the doctrine and practice of Mass sacrifice. The 'wherefore' (in Latin, *unde*) in the middle is crucial. As Oliver O'Donovan rightly concludes, the 'cardinal assertion of Article 31' is that 'there is no *other* grace available to mankind than that offering once made...Our salvation is wrought for us in the death and resurrection of a first-century man – not strung out week by week in ritual representation through history.'[170] This emphasis can be seen in Thomas Cranmer's other works too. He asserts, for example, that,

> They say, that the mass is a sacrifice satisfactory for sin... but the only host and satisfaction for all the sins of the world is the death of Christ, and the oblation of his body upon the cross, that is to say, the oblation that Christ himself offered once upon the cross, and never but once, nor never any but he. And therefore that oblation which the priests make daily in their papistical masses, cannot be a satisfaction for other men's sins... but it is a mere illusion.[171]

It would therefore be irresponsible to handle half of Article 31 as if it thoughtfully reflected a doctrine of universal atonement. Cranmer's concern is to show us that there is only one place to go if we want satisfaction for all our sins, and that a merely human priest plays no part in offering for either our original or our actual sins. This was not an unusual interpretation of 1 John 2:2 (the text lying behind the emphasis on 'sins of the whole world' in the Article). William Tyndale, for example, in his exposition of 1 John (1531) also stresses that Christ's satisfaction was for both original and actual sins and 'that his blood is the satisfaction only.' Yet Tyndale says a number of times that Christ saves *his people* from their sins, and explains that 1 John 2:2 refers to a propitiation *for those who believe*. It was 'for all the sins of the world; both of theirs that went before, and of theirs that come after *in the faith*' (my emphasis). Indeed, he explains further that:

---

[170] O'Donovan, *On The 39 Articles* (Carlisle: Paternoster, 1986), p 125.

[171] See for example *The Writings and Disputations of Thomas Cranmer* (Cambridge, 1844), 1: p 81.

Christ is a full contenting, satisfaction and ransom for our sins: and not for ours only, which are apostles and disciples of Christ while he was yet here; or for ours which are Jews, or Israelites, and the seed of Abraham; or for ours that now believe at this present time, but for all men's sins, both for their sins which went before and believed the promises to come, and for ours which have seen them fulfilled, and also for all them which shall afterward believe unto the world's end, of whatsoever nation or degree they be.[172]

In his view, then, 1 John 2:2 is not about a propitiation for the reprobate. Like Cranmer and Article 31, he considers the cross to be sufficient for all,[173] but Tyndale is clear that 'Christ's blood only putteth away all the sin that ever was, is, or shall be, from *them that are elect.*' He speaks of how believers are 'elect unto the fellowship of the blood of Christ.' We are hence 'beloved of God, *more than the world*' and enjoy 'the favour of God, *which is not in the world.*'[174] He never unambiguously refers to what he would call 'Turks, Saracens, and heathen' as if they were purchased by Christ's blood.[175] Yet his view of the particularity of redemption and of 1 John 2:2 would not

---

[172] See Henry Walter (ed.), *The Works of William Tyndale: Volume 2* (Cambridge: Cambridge University Press, 1849), pp 154-157. He adds that 1 Timothy 2 is about '*some* of all nations and all degrees, and not the Jews only' (my emphasis).

[173] Henry Walter (ed.), *The Works of William Tyndale: Volume 3* (Cambridge: Cambridge University Press, 1850), p 177 ('once done for all', i.e. in no need of repetition by or for anyone) and 2: pp 196 and 265 (echoing Lombard). Tyndale's contemporary, John Bradford (1510-1555) also utilised the 'sufficient for all, but effectual to none but to the elect only' formula in his 'Defence of Election.' He was clear (alluding to John 17:9) that 'for whom he "prayed not," for them he died not.' See *The Writings of John Bradford* (Cambridge: Cambridge University Press, 1848), 1: p 320.

[174] Henry Walter (ed.), *The Works of William Tyndale: Volume 1* (Cambridge: Cambridge University Press, 1848), p 72 (my emphasis). 'Christ's blood only putteth away... from them that are elect' may possibly mean his blood *alone* is what covers our sin (see his use of only and alone in *Works* 2: p 188). In 3: p 192, however, the application of redemption (the opening of our eyes to accept it) is merited *for the elect.*

[175] Those who benefit savingly from Christ's blood are servants of Christ (2: p 140; 3: pp 57-59), those who believe (2: p 159), men considered as a creaturely race (2: pp 325-326; 3:77, 193), the poor (3: p 83), those who repent (3: p 31), the elect (3: p 35), all degrees of human (3: p 109). Though see also *Works* 2: pp 29, 36; 3: p 126 on some who perish.

have prevented him affirming words like those in Article 31 which, in that historical context, perfectly reflect his emphasis on the utter and unique sufficiency of Christ's satisfaction for sin.[176]

The context should not be ignored when interpreting any text, a point of even greater importance when it is also noted that this Article comes in the section (Articles 25-31) devoted to the sacraments and not, for instance, in the section on salvation (Articles 11-18) where soteriological concerns are concentrated. Cardinal Newman ran aground on this very Article in his Tract 90 when he insisted that the Roman Catholic 'sacrifice of the mass' was not being rejected here because 'sacrifices of Masses' was plural. In the end he realised the impossibility of that interpretation and left the Church of England for Rome. I would not counsel advocates of universal atonement to do that, of course, but it would be safer for them not to place so much weight on an equally implausible interpretation of Article 31.

This stress on the sufficiency of the atonement is also characteristic of the other Anglican formularies. The Homilies, for example, in preaching the cross, present it as sufficient to pay the ransom for all who truly believe in Christ:

> Christ, by his one oblation and once offering of himself upon the cross, hath taken away our sins, and hath restored us again into God's favour, so fully and perfectly, that no other sacrifice for sin shall hereafter be requisite or needful in all the world.[177]

> Christ is now made the righteousness of all them that truly do believe in him. He for them paid their ransom by his death.

---

[176] There are a few places where Tyndale seems to equate creation and redemption in their universality. For example, he says in *Works*, 2: p 172 that one's brother is 'the image of God and price of Christ's blood' (see that same pattern in *Works*, 1: pp 26, 299, 464, 470; 2: pp 11, 56, 63, 126, 207, 325-326; 3: pp 6, 57-59, 183, 200). I think the best interpretation of this almost clichéd phrase in Tyndale would take account of the fact that he is talking about *Christian* neighbours (at least, baptised neighbours in a Christian country, 'brethren' ['my brethren, all God's elect', 2: p 170] or 'brothers'), and alluding to 1 Corinthians 8:11, Romans 14:15, or 1 John 4:10-11, 20-21.

[177] Book II: 'The Second Homily concerning the Death and Passion of our Saviour Christ.'

He for them fulfilled the Law in his life...[178]

> So pleasant was this sacrifice and oblation of his Son's death,
> which he so obediently and innocently suffered, that he would
> take it for the only and full amends for all the sins of the world.
> And such favour did he purchase, by his death, of his heavenly
> Father for us, that, for the merit thereof – if we be true
> Christians indeed, and not in word only – we be now fully in
> God's grace again, and clearly discharged from our sin.[179]

The clear stress here is on the uniqueness and universal sufficiency
of the cross for all who truly believe, in the same polemical
atmosphere where some were claiming other satisfactions for sin
were available. A definite atonement, not one which puts us merely
into a saveable state, is hereby presented. Homily I on the Passion
stresses the cross as paying 'our debt' and discharging 'us' from it,
which again sounds very much like a definite atonement. The end of
Cranmer's 'Fruitful Exhortation to the reading and Knowledge of
Holy Scripture' at the start of the Homilies speaks of Christ 'that died
for us all,' but I think this forms a prayer-wish on behalf of believers
in the church, not a doctrinal statement about the universal extent of
the atonement.

There are two other potentially ambiguous lines in the
Homilies which could be used on the other side of the argument.
They are both in 'The Second Homily concerning the Death and
Passion of our Saviour Christ' in Book II. First, the sermon speaks of
Christ as 'suffering death universally for all men' and then later
exhorts the congregation thus: 'O sinful man... Did Christ suffer his
passion for thee, and wilt thou shew no compassion towards him?'
The ambiguity is in whether this latter exhortation is addressing an
unconverted man, or a sinful Christian. If it is definitely the former
then this could be cited as an instance of an appeal based on an
'unlimited' atonement.

However, given the more consistent stress on the *sufficiency*
of the cross in the formularies generally, and the way in which all

---

[178] Book I: Homily 3 'Of the Salvation of all Mankind.' See also the use of Hebrews
10:14 in this homily.
[179] Book II: 'Of the Passion: for Good-Friday.'

listeners are usually assumed to be professing (though sinful) Christians, I think it would be best to interpret these phrases in line with that broader picture. If anyone is minded to do otherwise then there should at least be a recognition of the tentative nature of such a conclusion and the weight of evidence on the other side. As far as the Homilies are concerned, the cross seems to have been specifically designed: 'The end of his coming was to save and deliver his people' says the Homily on the Nativity.[180]

Turning back to the Articles, Article 17 is more clearly focused on the issue of predestination and God's eternal plan, stating that:

> Predestination to life is the everlasting purpose of God, whereby, before the foundations of the world were laid, He hath constantly decreed by His counsel secret to us, to deliver from curse and damnation those whom He hath chosen in Christ out of mankind, and to bring them by Christ to everlasting salvation as vessels made to honour.

There is no explicit mention of the debate between limited and unlimited accounts of the atonement here. It may however be legitimate for us to ask which would be more consistent with the tenor of this Article. What it appears to teach is that in eternity God chose a group of people and then worked out their deliverance from 'curse and damnation' so he could bring them to 'everlasting salvation.' 'Those whom He hath chosen' are those who are delivered from curse and damnation (presumably by the cross). Those delivered from damnation are those who are brought to everlasting salvation. This is focused, intentional redemption. The cross does what the decree designed.

There is no mention in Article 17 of a conditional or hypothetical universalism, only of the salvation of the chosen. It is stressed, however, that who those 'chosen' are remains a mystery to us (it is part of 'His counsel secret to us'), which leaves the way open for a universal proclamation of the gospel. An Arminian spin on this Article would be strained beyond credibility. It is possible to make a case that a Calvinistic hypothetical universalism reading would be

---

[180] See Toplady, *Complete Works*, p 653 for a discussion of the Homilies on particular redemption.

somewhat contrived, though it is not ruled out *per se*. Nevertheless, definite atonement, while not spoken of explicitly here, is at least fully consistent with how the Article describes God's plan.

Historically, there was an attempt in 1595 to clarify the Articles of Religion in an even more explicitly Calvinist direction. This failed in England, although the nine so-called Lambeth Articles were later incorporated into the Irish version of the articles by Archbishop Ussher.[181] These Lambeth Articles did not, however, contain an explicit statement on limited atonement,[182] and Ussher himself leaned towards hypothetical universalism.[183] Proposals from Bishop Carleton and others in the 1620s that the Canons of Dort be formally established as authoritative in the Church of England were not followed through.[184] But as Bishop Thomas Barlow (1608/9-1691) put it, 'did not the Church of England, and all her obedient sons till 1626 or 1628 (both the universities) approve the doctrine of that synod?'[185] Augustus Toplady would have agreed. He adduces copious amounts of evidence in his *Historic Proof of the Doctrinal Calvinism of the Church of England* (1774) to prove that the following bishops and clergy are among those who held to definite atonement, and definitely not to the indefinite universal atonement scheme of the Arminians: Ridley, Latimer, Bucer, Rowland Taylor, Thomas Causton and Thomas Higbed, John Careless, John Bradford, John Melvin,

---

[181] On the Lambeth Articles see Schaff, *The History of Creeds*, pp 658-662. On the Irish Articles (and their pedigree as 'the chief basis of the Westminster Confession') see pp 662-665. According to Fuller (as cited in Schaff, p 661), Dr. Reynolds also attempted to get the Lambeth Articles into the Prayer Book at the Hampton Court Conference of 1604.

[182] For the text of the Articles see Schaff, *The Evangelical Protestant Creeds* (Grand Rapids: Baker, 1996), pp 523-524.

[183] Godfrey, 'Reformed Thought', p 169 says, 'Although the term is anachronistic, Ussher's views on the atonement... must be called Amyraldian.' See his *The Judgement of the Late Archbishop of Armagh* (London, 1658) and the exposition in Moore, *English Hypothetical Universalism*, pp 173-186.

[184] See Milton, *The British Delegation*, p 381 and the details in Tyacke, *Anti-Calvinists*, pp 152 and 176-177. Carleton himself opposed universal atonement, denying that it was 'a truth of the Scripture, or the doctrine of the Church of England'; Toplady, *Complete Works*, p 245 note d.

[185] MS marginalia, p 7 of John Goodman, *A Serious and Compassionate Inquiry*, 1674, Bodl. Oxf., 8° A 43 Linc. See John Spurr, 'Barlow, Thomas (1608/9–1691)', *Oxford Dictionary of National Biography* (Oxford: Oxford University Press, 2004).

Andrew Willet, and the British Delegation to the Synod of Dort.[186] Toplady himself was a staunch proponent of particular redemption, and often defended its Anglican credentials against those, such as John Wesley, who attacked it.[187]

The Westminster Divines were originally charged not with writing their own Confession but with amending the *Thirty-nine Articles*, to 'clear and vindicate them', that is, protect them from false interpretations. Despite their clear Calvinism, they left Article 2's statement 'for all actual sins of men' and Article 15's allusion to John 1:29 ('sins of the world') untouched. This probably indicates that they were not generally read as being statements about unlimited atonement and could easily bear a Reformed interpretation. After the Restoration in 1660 when 'Arminianism returned as a flood'[188] the Church of England reverted to the *Thirty-nine Articles* without change in an Arminian direction or any further clarification, despite the anti-puritan nature of that settlement and almost a century of further theological debate since they were first devised.[189] Thus the Articles have never been officially amended either explicitly to include or to exclude limited atonement.

In 1968, however, a Report of the Archbishops' Commission on Christian Doctrine not only recommended abolition of subscription to the Articles, but suggested changes to the text itself.[190] Some of these are relevant to the issues here. For example, the end of Article 2 was to be rephrased so as to present Christ's work as being 'to reconcile the world to God, and to be a sacrifice for all sins of men.' This changes the focus of the atonement from being God-centred to being man-centred (the original says 'to reconcile his Father to us'), as if the problem was merely us and our sin, and not the righteous wrath of God against us. It also removes reference to original sin and the distinction between that and actual sins, which could be a step in a Pelagian direction. Because it removes the

---

[186] Toplady, *Complete Works*, pp 132, 141-143, 150-151, 166, 168, 174, 181, 191 note u, 221, 245.

[187] See my *The True Profession of the Gospel*, pp 82-85, 88-90, 102-104.

[188] Toplady, *Complete Works*, p 278.

[189] On the Restoration Settlement see Lee Gatiss, *The Tragedy of 1662: The Ejection and Persecution of the Puritans* (London: Latimer Trust, 2007), pp 12-23.

[190] *Subscription and Assent to the Thirty-nine Articles* (London: SPCK, 1968).

reference to 'us' and exchanges it for 'the world,' however, it does appear to make the Article much more susceptible to an Arminian interpretation than the original.

The revisers make their views even clearer in their Article 3, which reads, 'Salvation through Christ is intended by God for all men in all ages.' This adds a stress on God's intention which was not present previously, and takes a clearly Arminian view on the subject. Sufficiency for all men in all ages would be one thing; but efficacious divine intention for all would have been quite another. Furthermore, Article 17 of the original Articles is entirely mangled by the revisers' suggested Article 13, entitled 'The purpose of God' or 'God's plan' (there are two options presented). This begins by asserting that 'God wills/wants all men to be saved,' and removes all the strong and clear statements we have on predestination, replacing them instead with ambiguous and Romanising sentiments regarding baptism. We surely must be grateful to God that these revised Articles remained and remain only suggestions.

So what can we conclude as regards the official standards of the Church of England on the subject of limited atonement? Herman Bavinck, a sharp-sighted theologian with no particular axe to grind as far as Anglicanism is concerned, concluded that 'The Anglican confession is silent on the subject.'[191] The formularies certainly seem to make no definitive statement either for or against it *per se*, nor should we necessarily expect them to. Their ambivalence allows a certain breadth of views within a generally Reformed framework, and it remains debateable how consistent different views of the atonement would be within that system. The formularies do, however, very clearly declare the utter sufficiency of Christ's work on the cross for the salvation of everyone who believes, and they are opposed to what became known as Arminianism.

---

[191] Bavinck, *Reformed Dogmatics*, 3: p 460.

4. PRACTICAL CONCLUSIONS

Some appear to think that if the use of a doctrine or the difference it makes practically is not immediately apparent then the doctrine itself cannot be that important. While rejecting this elevation of the pragmatic (because we must always take care to speak truly and accurately of our holy God, regardless of any superficially apparent implications), it is eminently true that all doctrine is practical. We have already seen how the scope or intent of Christ's atonement is a question that is intimately related to the nature of what he has done for us; and to get the latter wrong can create a whole host of pastoral problems. If Christ did not come to save but only to make salvation possible, much about being a Christian becomes contingent on me and my free will. In addition, many spiritual ailments are less susceptible to treatment by the diluted medicine of an indefinite, universal atonement.

On the other hand, in his excellent book *Atonement Matters*, Tom Barnes ends by saying that he is 'convinced that Definite Atonement is one of the best supplements which the body of Christ can drink down to reverse its weariness and strengthen its bones and muscles.'[1] He unpacks how definite atonement strengthens the church's glorification of God, its understanding of salvation, its assurance of God's love, its faith and hope in God, its sense of transformation, and its evangelism and mission. As was also noted recently in the *Wall Street Journal* of all places, churches holding to particular redemption are no less engaged in their communities, even in social action to help the poor.[2]

---

[1] T. Barnes, *Atonement Matters: A Call to Declare the Biblical View of the Atonement* (Darlington: Evangelical Press, 2008), pp 287-288.

[2] Aaron Belz, 'How Calvinists Spread Thanksgiving Cheer: Charity and predestination go hand in hand,' in *The Wall Street Journal*, November 18th 2011 notes that the generous church he writes about has a 'theologically conservative raison d'être,' and, 'is committed to Reformation doctrines such as total depravity (every person is born sinful) and limited atonement (salvation is available only to the elect).' He concludes that 'These beliefs are typically regarded as ugly and inhumane by American culturati,' and yet after examining the actions of a church which believed them, he concluded that such teachings 'provide a basis for hope.'

Various applications and implications have already been touched on in previous chapters. There are two particularly practical areas of ministry, however, in which this doctrine is especially important and strengthening: evangelism and assurance. With a look at these, and a concluding reflection on the whole debate, we draw this study to a close.

4.1. Evangelism

Some find it surprising that one can be a 'five point Calvinist' and also believe in evangelism. Yet Calvinists have consistently rejected as a perversion any view that restricts gospel preaching. Calvinists do not remove the Parable of the Sower, and its promiscuous sowing of the seed of God's word, from their Bibles. As Jim Packer rightly says, 'a Christian should evangelize better – more earnestly, more tirelessly, more expectantly – for being a Calvinist!'[3] Reformed evangelists offer to people Christ and his perfect, completed salvation as a gift, not just the mere possibility of salvation on yet another lifelong treadmill. George Whitefield thought therefore that predestination and particular redemption have

> a natural tendency to rouse the soul... Whereas universal redemption is a notion sadly adapted to keep the soul in its lethargic sleepy condition.[4]

As the excellent Getty-Townend song puts it, the church must arise, put its armour on and reach out to those in darkness, with the confidence that 'When faced with trials on ev'ry side, We know the outcome is secure, And Christ will have the prize for which he died – an inheritance of nations.'[5]

Yet this does not comport well with a common theory of evangelism which sees the essential message of the gospel as 'Christ died for

---

[3] See J.I. Packer, 'A Calvinist – and an Evangelist!' in *The Collected Shorter Writings of J. I. Packer* (Carlisle: Paternoster, 1998), 2: p 209. Ken Stewart's article at http://www.thegospelcoalition.org/publications/34-1/calvinism-and-missions-the-contested-relationship-revisited/ shows that it is simply not the case that Calvinists have neglected world mission.

[4] From his letter to John Wesley in A. Dallimore, *George Whitefield* Volume 2 (Edinburgh: Banner of Truth, 1980), p 560.

[5] 'O Church, Arise.' Words and Music by Keith Getty & Stuart Townend. Copyright © 2005 Thankyou Music.

you.' It is attachment to this theory of gospel presentation which probably lies behind some objections to limited atonement. So, for example, R.T. Kendall insists that unlimited atonement is the correct doctrine and that it does matter – 'I can say to anybody, "Christ died for you". In our evangelism this makes a real difference: certainly to the evangelist if not also to the person we are trying to reach for Christ.'[6] No less than four times in his short section on limited atonement, David Broughton Knox also appeals to this formula: Preachers should be at liberty, he says, and indeed are obliged, to press home the gospel offer by saying to each sinner, 'Christ died for you';[7] it is improperly restrictive to deny the propriety of laying on the conscience of the unconverted their duty to repent because Christ died for them;[8] in fact 'all may be told 'Christ has died for you; therefore accept the proffered salvation'';[9] whereas limited atonement 'blunts the point of evangelism in preventing the pressing home of the claims of Christ on the consciences of the hearer, by interdicting such phrases as "Christ died for you."'[10]

Clearly it is a point of no small importance for Kendall, Knox, and others that a preacher can and should move the conscience of unbelievers to accept Christ by telling them that he died for them. Their desire to safeguard and promote effective evangelism is of course highly laudable. But is such pathos in evangelism recommended by the example or command of the earliest gospel preachers? Is the emotive plea to the conscience to accept salvation because it was won at so high a price as the death of Jesus a biblical method of winning souls?

William Cunningham had no hesitation in saying that appealing to people on such a basis is, 'a mode of preaching the gospel never adopted by our Lord and His apostles'.[11] A cursory glance at the evangelistic speeches in Acts, for example, reveals that this technique was never (so far as is recorded) employed by the apostles, or men such as Stephen or Philip so effective in preaching. The sermons and speeches in Acts all have their distinctive marks,

---

[6] Kendall, *Calvin and English Calvinism*, p viii.
[7] Knox, 'Some Aspects', p 261.
[8] *Ibid.*, p 263.
[9] *Ibid.*, p 264.
[10] *Ibid.*, p 266.
[11] Cunningham, *Historical Theology*, 2: p 345.

and yet the essential core of the message appears to be, 'Christ is risen, and is appointed as Lord and Judge, so repent.' We look in vain for 'Christ has died for you; therefore accept the proffered salvation' among the speeches in Acts.

The cross is obviously not absent from a proclamation about a *risen* Messiah (how and perhaps why he first died seems an obvious detail to include). It clearly formed part of the early gospel message; as 1 Corinthians 15:3 makes clear, it is of primary importance 'that Christ died for our sins.' Yet it is not necessarily the focal point of every apostolic proclamation, which we might imagine it should be if we had only read 1 Corinthians 2:2 ('I resolved to know nothing among you but Jesus Christ and him crucified'). Still less is an unlimited atonement made the basis for an appeal to the conscience for acceptance. Indeed, the conscience of Peter's hearers is cut to the quick (Acts 2:37), just as some of Paul's Athenian audience were no doubt arrested to hear of their impending judgment by Jesus (Acts 17:31). Neither are told 'Christ died for you' and the response called for on each occasion was not 'accept the proffered salvation', or 'love God back', but simply 'repent!'[12]

This is evangelism as patterned for us by the apostles and recorded by Luke. The absence of the shibboleth, 'Christ died for you', or of an explanation of the mechanics of the atonement may come as a surprise, since preaching which has included such things has in the recent past been greatly used by God. But it cannot claim a straightforward mandate from the scriptures, or be insisted on as a *sine qua non* of true biblical evangelism.[13] 1 Corinthians 15:14 does not say that our preaching is useless without an unlimited atonement. So what should we make of this kind of evangelism? Grudem avers,

> I do not think we should rush to criticize an evangelist who tells an audience of unbelievers, 'Christ died for your sins,' if it is made clear in the context that it is necessary to trust in Christ before one can receive the benefits of the gospel offer.[14]

---

[12] On apostolic preaching in Acts see L. Gatiss, 'The Evangelistic Sermons in Acts' at http://www.theologian.org.uk/bible/acts-sermons.html.

[13] See Van Genderen and Velema, *Concise Reformed Dogmatics*, p 528: 'It is not, however, the mandate of the church to tell everyone: Christ has died in your place.'

[14] Grudem, *Systematic Theology*, p 602.

We should not, of course, *ever* rush into criticism, especially if people merely 'unreflectively use ambiguous language.'[15]

Thinking more widely, Reformed theologians do affirm that the world is different as a result of the cross, even if that does not mean the whole world is saved as a result. There are benefits given indiscriminately to everyone as a result of what Christ did, not least the introduction of 'many uplifting moral influences into the world.'[16] In that sense Jesus' death has benefited the whole world of elect and non-elect alike. More specifically, anyone who comes into contact with 'the message of the cross,' even if they do not perseveringly and savingly believe it, may receive some blessings by it. It is a gift and a blessing for an individual or society to be enlightened in any way by the light of the gospel, and it may have many positive influences, for example, in the realms of thought, art, and behaviour.

Particularly within the visible church, some who are not elect may taste of the goodness of the world to come (Hebrews 6:4-5). As the Canons of Dort say, God confers on those who are outwardly called by the gospel 'various gifts,' but many refuse to come or bear fruit and for this 'the fault lies in themselves.'[17] They may experience some temporary growth and joy as a result of the seed of the word, like the green shoots that grew at first in Jesus' Parable of the Sower, but then were either scorched or choked. These blessings owe their power in some way to the cross, which is at the heart of the Christian faith. What's more, the angels, and even creation itself are affected by the salvation of the elect through the cross, though that is not of course the same as saying Christ died *for* them.[18]

Some Reformed theologians would go further. Charles Hodge says, 'Augustinians do not deny that Christ died for all men. What they

---

[15] *Ibid.,* p 602 n45. Cf. the stronger prohibition on this language in Feenstra, *Unspeakable Comfort*, p 83.

[16] Boettner, *The Reformed Doctrine,* p 160. Cf. books such as A.J. Schmidt, *Under the Influence: How Christianity Transformed Civilisation* (Grand Rapids: Zondervan, 2001) or J. Kennedy and J. Newcombe, *What if Jesus had Never Been Born? The Positive Impact of Christianity in History* (Nashville: Thomas Nelson, 2001).

[17] Canons 3/4.9.

[18] For a profound meditation on further effects of the cross beyond the elect (to unbelievers, irrational creatures, and even angels), see Bavinck, *Reformed Dogmatics,* 3: pp 470-475.

deny is that He died equally, and with the same design, for all men.'[19] So, as far as 'Christ died for you' language is concerned, 'we do not reply to the Arminian tenet with an unqualified negative,' says Loraine Boettner. 'But what we do maintain ,' he continues, 'is that the death of Christ had special reference to the elect in that it was effectual for their salvation, and that the effects which are produced in others are only incidental to this one great purpose.'[20] Grace overflows within the bounds of the covenant people, the visible church, even if it does not finally save outside the bounds of God's elective purpose.

Yet I am not convinced that this is an adequate basis for the 'Christ died for you, so come to him' method of evangelism. If it is without an explicit biblical sanction would it not be better to rethink it, however personally attached to it we might be? Its undoubted effectiveness in former times may, in any case, be due more to cultural factors than we care to admit. Telling people that 'Christ died for you' may have had a particularly compelling significance for the post-World War II generation, for whom the idea of people laying down their lives for others was not merely a platitude but often an evocative and tender memory.

There may also be something deeper than that. Archbishop Rowan Williams recently said that Britain was a society 'uncomfortably haunted by the memory of religion,' and that it was not quite sure what to do about it.[21] Doug Wilson suggested some years ago a possible reason for this:

> When many individuals in a culture have received the mark of baptism, the presence of this obligation works its way out into the cultural assumptions held in common by all. And this is how a culture can come to be very wicked, and yet be, to use Flannery O Conner's phrase, Christ-haunted... Oddly, many unbelievers have a better sense of this than we do. They know that a claim of Christ rests upon them – they feel the weight of it.

---

[19] Hodge, *Systematic Theology*, 2: p 558. See also Murray, 'The Atonement and the Free Offer', pp 64-65.

[20] Boettner, *The Reformed Doctrine*, p 161.

[21] Reported in *The Telegraph* and *Guardian* newspapers on 22nd and 23rd March 2009.

They want to ignore this claim, but it still presses on them.[22]

In such a context, appealing to the conscience to 'accept the Christ who died for you' may have a very powerful effect on those haunted by the unexplored but weighty obligation of their baptism and church membership. In previous generations, this variant on the Moral Influence theory of the atonement may have warmed the hearts of those with the stiffest upper lips and helped to give them assurance of God's love, helping them to take the first steps of faith. In the same way, many unbelievers in the past have been stirred by the evangelistic use of Revelation 3:20 and the knocking of Christ on the door of their hearts, despite the fact that this text in its context is clearly addressed to existing members of a church, to rouse them from complacency, not to outsiders *per se*.[23] Yet it has been successful precisely because many intuitively felt the significance of their at least nominal membership of an established national church.

Yet as the ghost of nominal Christianity is driven out by a post-modern secularism which cares very little for Jesus and whether he loves us or not, perhaps such a strategy has had its day. We must find new methods of declaring the old truth that 'he is able to save completely those who come to God through him' (Hebrews 7:25), which are as faithful as possible to the Bible's witness concerning the effectiveness and sufficiency of the cross. For instance, 'he died to pay for sin' or 'the cross was for sinners like you and me' or 'his death is sufficient for you' or 'he has done everything necessary to save us,' or 'whoever believes in Christ will be completely saved by his blood' all stress the completeness of his work without becoming unhelpfully enmeshed in this more nuanced debate. They also ensure that the centre of gravity in our proclamation remains Christ and his work, rather than shifting it towards the Christian and making our response determinative for everything.

---

[22] D. Wilson, *Mother Kirk: Essays and Forays in Practical Ecclesiology* (Moscow, Idaho: Canon Press, 2001), pp 97-98.

[23] On the evangelistic employment of this text see the chapter on 'Reaching a Decision' in John Stott's classic, *Basic Christianity* (IVP: Leicester, 1971 [1958]), pp 122-124 where he confesses it helped him as a seeker to understand the step of faith. See also the very helpful contextual correction in J. Chapman, *Know and Tell the Gospel: Help for the Reluctant Evangelist* (St. Matthias Press: Sydney, 1981), pp 169-171.

We ought to give thought to the way in which we present the cross evangelistically. We must take care that we do not misrepresent what Christ has done or cause ourselves theological difficulties further down the line. Besides, as Campbell Morgan reminds us, 'Men will not be saved by understanding the atonement. Men will not be saved by explaining the mystery of the resurrection. Men will not be saved by explaining the mystery of how the Spirit comes. They will just be saved by yielding to the Lord Christ. In the moment of yielding, he makes over to them all the virtues and values.'[24] It is the Lordship of Christ, demonstrated also in his resurrection and ascension, which gives us the authority to call everyone to repent and become his disciples (Matthew 28:18-20), and it is that Lordship which lies at the heart of our proclamation.

Arminius suggested that we ought not to be afraid to use the Bible's own universal language about the cross, such as in 1 John 2:2 or John 1:29. 'He who rejects such phraseology,' he wrote, 'is a daring man, one who sits in judgment on the Scriptures and is not an interpreter of them... The words themselves ought to be simply approved, because they are the words of Scripture.'[25] This sounds pious and humble. Surely we can just say what the text says, without qualification or fine distinctions?

Yet consider the confusion and misunderstanding which might occur if we applied this rule of evangelism to James 2:24 - 'a person is justified by works and not by faith alone.' Or when did you last hear an evangelistic sermon which repeated the clear biblical teaching of 1 Peter 3:21 that 'baptism... now saves you'? Surely we ought not to be afraid of saying to seekers and those on the fringe of the church, 'Whoever eats my flesh and drinks my blood has eternal life' (John 6:54)? Or perhaps, rather, we should be careful! We can (and must) approve such words as God's words. We should not reject his teaching, but we should be wary about wielding the sword of his word without great care. We cannot naively assume these words will be immediately understood in the way they were originally intended. One can use the precise words of scripture and yet lead people astray, and the context in which words are used is often key. We must

---

[24]   See G. Campbell Morgan, *Evangelism* (London: Henry Walter, 1964), pp 22-23.
[25]   *Writings*, 1: pp 316-317.

remember what Bassanio declares in Shakespeare's *Merchant of Venice*, 'In religion, what damnèd error, but some sober brow will bless it, and approve it with a text, hiding the grossness with fair ornament' (Act III, Scene II).

We should then, continue to evangelise and reach out to the lost with the glorious gospel of salvation. Those who are convinced of the truth of limited atonement need have no hesitations in doing so. The seventeenth century theologian, commentator, and pastor John Owen is often considered one of the staunchest Calvinists, especially on the death of Christ. Yet hear his appeal to the unconverted in his 'exhortation to such as are strangers to Christ,' where he calls out to them:

> This is somewhat of the word which he now speaks unto you: Why will ye die? why will ye perish? why will you not have compassion on your own souls? Can your hearts endure, or can your hands be strong, in the day of wrath that is approaching? It is but a little while before all your hopes, your reliefs, and presumptions will forsake you, and leave you eternally miserable. Look unto me, and be saved;—come unto me, and I will ease you of all sins, sorrows, fears, burdens, and give rest unto your souls. Come, I entreat you;—lay aside all procrastinations, all delays;—put me off no more;— eternity lies at the door. Cast out all cursed, self-deceiving reserves;—do not so hate me as that you will rather perish than accept of deliverance by me.

> These and the like things doth the Lord Christ continually declare, proclaim, plead, and urge on the souls of sinners; as it is fully declared, Proverbs 1:20–33. He doth it in the preaching of the word, as if he were present with you, stood amongst you, and spake personally to every one of you.[26]

This is a personal, urgent, passionate, moving appeal, based on the open-handed generosity of God in Christ, the sort of generosity which should cause every believer to explode with gratitude for God's overwhelming and undeserved grace towards us, and which should powerfully draw others to know and love Christ as we do. We might

---

[26] *Works*, I: p 422. See also Bruce Hindmarsh, *John Newton and the English Evangelical Tradition* (Oxford: Clarendon Press, 1996), pp 158, 162-168 on Newton, who loved John Owen's sermons and also held to a form of limited atonement.

multiply examples of such evangelistic appeals from others such as George Whitefield and Charles Spurgeon. Calvinists do not have to become Arminians the moment they enter the pulpit! As the great evangelist Phillip Jensen rightly says, the advice to be a Calvinist on our knees and an Arminian in the pulpit is 'the thoughtless advice of pragmatism, declaring theology to be irrelevant to the work of ministry.' It insults both systems of thought and attempts to reconcile the irreconcilable in an illogical and unbiblical way.[27] Based on the picture of the redeemed multitudes in Revelation 5:9, however, the song 'Lion of Judah' puts it well: 'As the Father has told us, for these You have died, For the nations that gather before You;' and yet 'the ears of all men need to hear of the Lamb who was crucified.'[28]

4.2. Assurance

R.T. Kendall was concerned in his work on Calvinism that a proper ground of Christian assurance be found. When asked, 'How do I know Christ has died for me?' he thought it necessary to be able to reply 'he died for you because he died for everyone.' By rejecting limited atonement, this expedient was designed to prevent introspective questioning as to whether one was part of the elect group for which Christ died. However, as Paul Helm points out, all Kendall managed to do was relocate the question: if Kendall was correct about the true limitation being at the point of Christ's intercession, then the doubting church member would be taught to question, 'How do I know Christ is praying for me?'[29]

---

[27] See Phillip D. Jensen, 'Preaching our Theology,' at www.phillipjensen.com and 'An Arminian in the Pulpit' in *The Briefing* 380 (May 2010), p 23 where he says, 'you cannot cherrypick bits out of a theological system without creating a new — and, in this case – illogical and unbiblical alternative.'

[28] 'You're the Lion of Judah,' by Robin Mark © 1997 Daybreak Music Ltd.

[29] See Helm, *Calvin and the Calvinists*, p 50. Scottish theologian James Fraser developed a form of 'middle way' universal redemption specifically because he sought 'to discover more substantial grounds for personal assurance.' However, Hunter Bailey, '*Via Media Alia*: Reconsidering the Controversial Doctrine of Universal Redemption in the Theology of James Fraser of Brea (1639-1699)' (PhD thesis, University of Edinburgh, 2008), pp 215-216 concludes that this failed to solve such problems of conscience, and that all he did was change a doubter's question from 'Did Jesus die for me?' to '*For what reason* did Jesus die for me?' while simultaneously surrendering the strength of his otherwise particularist system.

Scripture, however, uses limited atonement as a comfort and encouragement to believers. We saw this previously when we examined Romans 8:32. It also applies the atonement with a specific reference to the elect, the church, even the individual (Galatians 2:20) to bolster our confidence, trust, and perseverance in godliness. Ultimately, say advocates of limited atonement, if Christ died for everyone indiscriminately then those passages which apply his death for his people as a particular comfort to those people lose their pastoral force. A doubting or despairing Christian may well ask, 'Why should I be reassured by the cross that he has a special love for *me* as a believer, when actually he died for everyone indiscriminately?'[30] The idea that 'Jesus died for me' has no assuring value if he died equally for multitudes who are now in hell.

As Sinclair Ferguson points out, the doctrine of unlimited atonement 'cuts the nerve of assurance of salvation based on the atonement. For if Christ's atonement was made for someone who is never saved by it, how can I look to it with confidence that I will be 'saved by his precious blood'?'[31] Helm agrees and asks,

> How can a person be satisfactorily assured that he is saved by believing in a Saviour who loves everyone, but whose love and whose death in the case of many is ineffective because it does not correspond with God the Father's electing purpose?[32]

Definite atonement is of greater practical use in pastoral ministry than alternatives. If people can be shown from scripture and delight in the fact that God had a particular, personal, and effective design in sending Jesus to do everything necessary for their salvation, then they can be liberated from fear of their own substandard religious performance. They can appropriate and appreciate the atonement, as something accomplished specifically for them as a person – he truly is 'My Jesus, my Saviour' – and they can put faith to work, secure in the finished work of Christ. We can rest, as an old hymn says, in 'the deep, deep love of Jesus' and in,

How he watches o'er his loved ones

---

[30]   See Turretin, *Institutes* 2.14.XIV.xl. Recently I was told by a rural minister friend that he had been asked this precise question by a parishioner (who had not read Turretin!).

[31]   S.B. Ferguson, 'Preaching the Atonement', p 439.

[32]   Helm, *Calvin and the Calvinists*, p 49.

> Died to call them all his own
> How for them he intercedeth
> Watcheth o'er them from the throne.[33]

As D. Clair Davis said, 'Jesus didn't die to open the door. He didn't die to give you some help. He didn't die to stir you up to make something of yourself. He did a lot more than that. He *saved* you from your sins. He set you free from your foolish unbelief, so that now you see him in his glory.'[34] That means that when trouble comes or we stumble, we can look to him, with whom we have been united, and know that since he died and rose *for us* he will not let us go, but complete what he began. Knowing my own sinful heart, I find this tremendously liberating and a source of endless comfort and overflowing joy, and can passionately sing,

> Crown him the Lord of life,
> who triumphed over the grave,
> And rose victorious in the strife
> for those he came to save.[35]

We do not forget the corporate nature of the atonement or the Christian life. He died for his flock, his people, his church:

> From heaven he came and sought her
> To be his holy bride;
> With his own blood he bought her
> And for her life he died.[36]

Yet limited atonement also allows us to glory in a 'warm and tender individualism,'[37] which rejoices in the truth that we are known by name and were redeemed by a personal, powerful God. Particular redemption assures us of our eternal safety in a way that the Arminian scheme, which demands my full, unrestrained contribution as a *sine qua non* of salvation, can never do. As Toplady put it in his hymn '*From Whence This Fear and Unbelief*':

---

[33] By London merchant Samuel Trevor Francis (1834-1925).

[34] 'Personal Salvation' in P.A. Lillback (ed.), *The Practical Calvinist: An Introduction to the Presbyterian and Reformed Heritage* (Fearn: Christian Focus, 2002), p 32.

[35] 'Crown him with many crowns' by Matthew Bridges (1800-1894) and Godfrey Thring (1823-1903).

[36] 'The Church's One Foundation' by Samuel John Stone (1839-1900).

[37] Gresham Machen, quoted in Reymond, *A New Systematic Theology*, p 683.

If thou hast my Discharge procur'd,
And freely in my Room endur'd
The whole of Wrath Divine:
Payment God cannot twice demand,
First at my bleeding Surety's hand,
And then again at mine.

Such is the assurance that a definite, efficacious atonement alone can bring. This is the kind of cross to which we can securely cling.

A rock climber who trusts a rope which is frayed at any point has no assurance that it will hold, and will soon be in peril. Thus it is for those who trust in a deficient cross, a conditional cross, which cannot hold our entire weight and bring us safely home. Salvation is not a bridge that goes part of the way across a ravine, leaving us to construct the remainder by means of our free will response (perhaps even with some divine assistance). The cross definitely bridges the gap all the way. Only a limited atonement, limited in extent or intent but not in saving power, can give us true assurance and confidence – the confidence of faith which declares, not 'he came for all and for their potential salvation,' but 'For us and for our salvation he came down from heaven.'

5. CONCLUDING REFLECTIONS

What shall we do with this profound and controversial doctrine? James I instructed the British delegation to the Synod of Dort, 'Your advise shall be to those Churches, that their Ministers do not deliver in the Pulpit to the people those things for ordinary doctrines, which are the highest points of Schooles, and not fitt for vulgar capacity, but disputable on both sides." Gregory the Great (540-604) gave similar advice in his pastoral rule, cautioning that 'it should be perceived by the preacher how to avoid dragging the mind of his hearer beyond its ability, lest, so to speak, the string of the soul, when stretched more than it can bear, should be snapped. For every deep thing should be covered before a multitude of hearers, and scarcely disclosed to the few."[2]

Luther and Erasmus argued over the same point. Erasmus would rather not have certain doctrines openly discussed before the 'common herd' or 'untutored multitude.'[3] Luther, on the other hand, was vehemently opposed to such self-censorship from preachers. 'Truth and doctrine must be preached always, openly, and constantly, and never accommodated or concealed... If, therefore, God has willed that such things should be openly spoken of and published abroad without regard to the consequences, who are you to forbid it?'[4] God had a saving purpose in revealing the truth about the human will in scripture: 'It is thus for the sake of the elect that these things are published, in order that being humbled and brought back to nothingness by this means they may be saved.'[5]

John Owen, while agreeing with Luther here, also added a word about prudence in deciding when and where to broach more difficult subjects, saying,

> That it ought to be the design of every faithful minister, in the course of his ministry, *to withhold nothing* from those

---

[1] 'Instructions of King James I to the delegates' in *The British Delegation*, p 93.
[2] *The Book of Pastoral Rule*, Part 3 chapter 39 in *Patrologia Latina* 77:0124a.
[3] G. Rupp & P.S. Watson, *Luther and Erasmus: Free Will and Salvation* (Philadelphia: Westminster Press, 1969), p 40.
[4] *Ibid.*, pp 132, 135.
[5] *Luther and Erasmus*, p 137.

committed unto his charge that belongs unto their edification, as do all things that are written in the Scripture, but to declare unto them "the whole counsel of God," so far as he himself hath attained (Acts 20:20, 27). To give times and seasons unto especial truths, doctrines, expositions, is committed unto his own prudence by Him by whom he is made an "overseer, to feed the church of God;" but his design in general is, to "keep back nothing that is profitable,"—as is the sense of all the Scripture, even in its most abstruse and difficult passages (2 Timothy 3:16).[6]

This is wise and helpful advice. True doctrine should never be hidden as if we were ashamed of things that God has taught us in his word. Yet it is potentially unedifying to use the ordinary means of grace, the regular preaching ministry, as a platform on which to carry out a theological battle between Calvinists, Arminians, and Amyraldians. There is a time and a place, and these more controversial and difficult doctrines should not become the everyday heartbeat of our ministry unless we wish to earn a reputation merely as a theological Rottweiler and produce congregations whose growth is stunted because they are forever drunk on strong drink but cannot digest bread and milk.[7]

While I am firmly convinced of the truthfulness and biblical faithfulness of the doctrine of limited atonement, it is also, as Grudem comments, 'a subject that almost inevitably leads to some confusion, some misunderstanding, and often some wrongful argumentativeness and divisiveness among God's people – all of which are negative pastoral considerations.'[8] I have experienced this myself on a number of occasions as I have been preparing this book. Mudslinging amongst evangelicals is always an unedifying spectacle, and should be avoided in public if at all possible, especially when the

---

[6] John Owen, *An Exposition of the Epistle to the Hebrews* (Edinburgh: Banner of Truth, 1991), 4: pp 551-552.

[7] See P. Althaus, *The Theology of Martin Luther* (Philadelphia: Fortress Press, 1966), p 285 on Luther's view of appropriate timing when it comes to drinking the strong drink of teaching on predestination. Cunningham, *Historical Theology*, 2: p 503 urges that the points on which we agree with other orthodox believers 'ought to occupy a more prominent place in the ordinary course of public instruction than those in which they differ from us.'

[8] Grudem, *Systematic Theology*, p 603.

disputed doctrine is not one of primary importance. A brotherly disagreement in a spirit of love and humility as we search the scriptures together is much more likely to 'win friends and influence people.'

There is sometimes wisdom in what our opponents say in debate. Some may accuse limited atonement of being the thin edge of the hyper-calvinist wedge; but on the other hand, many members of the Synod of Dort were agreed that those 'who rejected this doctrine tended toward the quicksand of Popery, Pelagianism, and Socinianism.'[9] We do need to be careful that, whichever position we hold, we do not slide down the dangerous slippery slope on either side. Calvinists can become cold towards evangelism, even if that is not a logical conclusion of their theology. 'Amyraldians' and other 'middle-way' advocates can adopt so many Arminian arguments and presuppositions in differentiating themselves on the atonement that they unwittingly become unorthodox in other areas.[10] As well as denying penal substitutionary atonement,[11] Arminians can slip into 'open theism', which styles itself as a more consistent version of Arminianism and shares many of its cardinal tenets. It is not at all unknown or uncommon for advocates of 'universal atonement' (whether of the Calvinist/Amyraldian or the Arminian variety) to drift into forms of universalism more generally (as we see with emergent church leader, Rob Bell and others).

'A little leaven, leavens the whole lump' – adopting unorthodox positions in one part of our theological system eventually has implications for the rest, whether we acknowledge them or not. Those who think of themselves as four or four-and-a-half point Calvinists may actually, by the standards of the Synod of Dort, be as entitled to all five petals of the TULIP as the strictest Genevan. But if

---

[9] W.R. Godfrey, 'Reformed Thought on the Extent of the Atonement to 1618', p 170. See also the historical note on Arminianism after the Synod of Dort in Schaff, *The History of Creeds*, pp 515-516.

[10] On a bigger scale, Macleod, 'Amyraldus Redivivus,' pp 227-229 argues that Amyraldianism opened the door to a greater degeneration into liberalism as far as Presbyterians were concerned.

[11] E.g. H. Orton Wiley, *Christian Theology* (Kansas City: Beacon Hill, 1959), II, pp 246-247 rejects penal substitution on the grounds that it must lead either to limited atonement or to universal salvation. The same logic is used by Roger Nicole, 'The Case for Definite Atonement', p 202 in support of limited atonement.

Reformed folks generally could do with being more tolerant and aware of shades of opinion within a generic Calvinism, such hypothetical universalists must also be very careful that they do not unwittingly swing the pendulum too far in the opposite direction as they seek to balance out perceived extremes in their brothers.

Whichever side of this debate one is on, it is at least certain that Christ did die for our Christian brothers and sisters on the other side of the argument! It is all too easy to forget this. We should conduct ourselves, therefore, in an appropriate manner when engaging in this family discussion. When it comes to disagreements amongst those who are generally Reformed in their outlook, there is adequate scope for us to disagree on the fine details of limited atonement.[12] Our attention ought to be on evangelism in the light of the immense challenges we face in presenting the truly saving doctrine of the cross to multitudes of lost people in our broken world; and also on defending that gospel from the parasitic liberalism which ever threatens to suck the life out of it.

May the last word go to Reformed Evangelical Anglican theologian, James Hervey (1714-1758). In his 'Reflections on a Flower-Garden,' he wrote,

> In a grove of tulips, or a knot of pinks, one perceives a difference in almost every individual. Scarce any two are turned and tinctured exactly alike. Each allows himself a little particularity in his dress, though all belong to one family: so that they are various, and yet the same. A pretty emblem this, of the smaller differences between Protestant Christians.[13]

Let us always be alert to the dangers of the unholy aroma of a different gospel, which will from time to time sneak in to share our soil. But may the differences between Reformed believers of various shades never obscure our shared witness to our common Lord and Saviour, Jesus Christ.

---

[12] It is worth noting John Owen's irenic comments in the preface he wrote to Edward Polhill's, *The Divine Will* (London, 1673), a book which defended hypothetical universalism against particular redemption: 'It is our duty to bear with each other in things circumstantial, or different explanations of the same Truth, when there is no incursion made upon the Principles we own.'

[13] J. Hervey, *Meditations and Contemplations* (London, 1748), pp 174-175.

For Further Reading

T. Barnes, *Atonement Matters: A Call to Declare the Biblical View of the Atonement* (Darlington: Evangelical Press, 2008)

J.D. Moore, *English Hypothetical Universalism: John Preston and the Softening of Reformed Theology* (Cambridge: Eerdmans, 2007)

A. Milton, *The British Delegation and the Synod of Dort (1618-1619)* (Woodbridge: Boydell Press, 2005)

C.E. Hill and F.A. James (eds.), *The Glory of the Atonement: Biblical, Theological, and Practical Perspectives* (Downers Grove IL: InterVarsity Press, 2004)

T.R. Schreiner & B.A. Ware (eds.), *Still Sovereign: Contemporary Perspectives on Election, Foreknowledge, and Grace* (Grand Rapids: Baker, 2000)

G.M. Thomas, *The Extent of the Atonement: A Dilemma for Reformed Theology from Calvin to the Consensus* (Carlisle: Paternoster, 1997)

C.H. Pinnock (ed.), *The Grace of God – The Will of Man: A Case for Arminianism* (Grand Rapids: Zondervan, 1989)

R. Olson, *Arminian Theology: Myths and Realities* (Downers Grove: IVP, 2006)

B.G. Armstrong, *Calvinism and the Amyraut Heresy: Protestant Scholasticism and Humanism in Seventeenth Century France* (Madison: University of Wisconsin Press, 1969)

Greg Forster, *The Joy of Calvinism: Knowing God's Personal, Unconditional, Irresistible, Unbreakable Love* (Wheaton: Crossway, 2012).

Shai Linne, 'Mission Accomplished' at http://www.youtube.com/watch?hl=en&v=hZ_jFO2VzRQ&gl=UK.

Names Index

Scripture Index

Latimer Publications

LATIMER PUBLICATIONS

LATIMER PUBLICATIONS

CPSIA information can be obtained at www.ICGtesting.com
Printed in the USA
BVOW08s0923201113

336805BV00003B/479/P